Interpreting the
UPANISHADS

ANANDA WOOD

First Edition 1996
Second Edition 1997
Third and Revised Edition 2009

Copyright 1996 by Ananda Wood

Credits: Cover Design by Red Sky Designs, Mumbai
Book Design by Ananda Wood

Published by: ZEN PUBLICATIONS
A Division of Maoli Media Private Limited
60, Juhu Supreme Shopping Centre,
Gulmohar Cross Road No. 9,
JVPD Scheme, Juhu,
Mumbai 400 049. India
Tel: +91 9022208074
eMail: info@zenpublications.com
Website: www.zenpublications.com

Prepared by: Ananda Wood
A-1 Ashoka, 3 Naylor Road,
Pune 411 001, India
eMail: woodananda@gmail.com

Ananda Wood is currently a moderator
on the Advaitin e-group. Most of his
books and articles may be accessed at
http://sites.google.com/site/advaitaenquiry/

ISBN-13 978-81-88071-52-4

Contents

Self

Happiness

The three states

The divine presence

Teacher and disciple

Preface

Do we know anything that is plainly and simply true, without any of the 'ifs' and 'buts' that complicate everything we perceive through our limited and uncertain personalities?

And is it thus possible to find any common basis of knowledge on which we can always rely, no matter what particular conditions and uncertainties surround our little bodies, senses and minds in a much larger universe?

The Upanishads are early texts that describe just such an enquiry into plain truth. However, there are two problems which complicate our understanding of these texts today.

First, they were composed at a time when knowledge was largely expressed in the imaginative metaphors of myth and ritual. Thus, along with their philosophical enquiry, the Upanishads also describe an archaic mythical and ritual context. It is from this archaic context that the enquiry was made, in times that are now long passed.

And second, as the founding texts of a very old philosophical tradition, they are expressed in a highly condensed way: which leaves them rather open to interpretation and explanation. The condensed statements of the Upanishads were called 'shruti' or 'heard'; because they were meant to be learned by hearing them directly from a living teacher, who would recite and interpret the words. Having received such a statement of condensed philosophical teaching, a student was meant to think about it over and over again, through a sustained process of individual reflection and enquiry. Eventually, after passing through many stages of thinking and rethinking the questions involved, the student was meant to come at last to a thorough and independent understanding of the statement, in his or her own right.

In the two and a half thousand years or more since the Upanishads began to be composed, their original statements have been interpreted and explained in many different ways, through many different schools of thought. Some schools have emphasized a religious approach to truth, through devotion to a worshipped God. Some schools have emphasized a mystical approach, through exercises of meditation that cultivate special states of experience beyond the ordinary limitations of our minds. And some schools emphasize a philosophical approach, through reasoned enquiry into common experience.

This book is focused on the philosophical approach. It follows Shrī Shankara's Advaita Vedānta tradition, as interpreted by Shrī Ātmānanda, a modern advaita philosopher who lived in Kerala State, India, 1883-1959.

The book asks how some ideas from the Upanishads can be translated into modern terms. This is a somewhat different approach from directly translating the texts. For each idea, selected passages have been translated and placed alongside much freer retellings that incorporate a fair degree of interpretation and commentary.

The retellings have been reproduced from a companion volume, called *From the Upanishads*. The abbreviation *FTU* refers to this companion volume, in page number references that show from where the retellings have been reproduced.

Hence this book and its companion volume form a pair, with cross-references between them. However, each volume can be read quite independently of the other.

Like the original texts, the book is perhaps best read as an anthology of collected passages. Because of their condensed expression, the Upanishads are meant to be thought about selectively, concentrating attention on one passage at a time. In various different passages, the same fundamental principles are approached again and again, in various different ways. Thus, one is free to pick out a particular passage that suits one's interests and one's state of mind at the time.

The trick is to avoid confusing the differing approaches through which the Upanishads ask different questions about one common truth. Then one can concentrate on those particular passages and those particular questions that hold one's attention sufficiently for the hard thinking that the subject requires.

'This' and 'that'

On the whole, the language of the Upanishads is simple. The main problems of interpretation do not come from any excessive complexity of grammar, nor from overly long and technical words. Since the language used is an early form of classical Sanskrit, there is sometimes a little trouble with the occasional archaic usage whose meaning may not be fully remembered; but this is relatively minor and peripheral.

The more basic problem comes from the philosophical character of the Upanishads. Their essential purpose is to stimulate reflection and enquiry. So they often raise questions about what words and concepts mean. This applies particularly to ordinary, common words like 'know' or 'be', or 'true' or 'real', or 'self' or 'world', or 'this' or 'that'. While the meaning of such words is open to question, so too is the interpretation of the Upanishads, which use these words in a way that puts them up for questioning.

In the peace invocation that is often placed at the beginning of the Brihadāraṇyaka and Īsha Upanishads, there is a striking example of simple language thus used to provoke thought. The language is so simple that it is possible to make a somewhat intelligible word for word translation of the relevant passage[1], with the order of the words unchanged:

pūrṇam adah pūrṇam idam	The full, that; the full, this.
pūrṇāt pūrṇam udacyate	From the full, the full arises.
pūrṇasya pūrṇam ādāya	Of the full, the full taken back,
pūrṇam evāvashishyate	the full alone remains.

Though just about intelligible, the translation is of course awkward. First, there is a problem of idiom. 'The full, that' is a common Sanskrit construction whose idiomatic equivalent in English is: 'That is the full.' Similarly, 'the full taken back' could be translated more idiomatically as 'when the full is taken back'. Second, by translating the word 'pūrṇam' too narrowly, as 'the full', the philosophical implications are not quite rightly conveyed. 'Pūrṇam' also means 'complete'. In the context of the Upanishads, this clearly

---

[1]Though often placed in the peace invocation at the beginning of the Brihadāraṇyaka and Īsha Upanishads, the passage may also be found in the Brihadāraṇyaka Upanishad 5.1.

refers to 'complete reality', which might be better translated as 'all'. So to try making the translation less awkward, perhaps it could be modified as follows:

> That is all. This is all.
> All arises out of all.
> Of all, when all is taken in,
> what remains is only all.

This is still quite a literal translation, and it is now in fluent English; but it has a problem of tone. At worst, it could be read as silly doggerel, showing up the absurdity of mystical philosophy. At best, it could be construed to have a tone of mocking irony, using a light-hearted facade to say something more profound. In neither case does it convey the philosophical tone of quiet certainty that is found in the original.

The trouble is that cryptic utterances like 'All arises out of all' are no longer taken seriously, in modern philosophical discussion. In fact, they are held up as glaring examples of 'trivial' or 'tautological' or 'woolly' or 'fuzzy' language, which serves as a cover for half-baked ideas that have not been properly questioned and tested. If anyone makes this kind of cryptic statement today, the immediate response, quite rightly, is that the speaker should explain further and be more specific about what is meant.

How does one try to solve this problem of tone in translating the simple, but sometimes cryptic statements of the Upanishads? There is a temptation to dress up the translation in strange or complicated language, to make it seem that hidden depths are lurking below; but this would be merely pretentious. The only way out is to make a specific interpretation; and to translate accordingly, perhaps adding some further explanation and commentary.

In the above passage from the peace invocation, the words 'that' and 'this' need more specific interpretation. So does the word 'pūrṇam', which is not quite adequately translated as 'the full' or as 'all'. In the retelling reproduced below (from *FTU*, page 42), the word 'that' is interpreted as the known world; the word 'this' is interpreted as the knowing self; and 'pūrṇam' is interpreted as complete reality, which is both knower and known. Accordingly, the passage is taken to describe reality as non-dual consciousness: underlying all mentally created divisions of experience into 'this' which knows and 'that' which is known. From underlying consciousness, all appearances of objects arise: as they are perceived by body, senses and mind. And back to this same consciousness, all appearances return: as they are understood and assimilated into knowledge.

> That world out there, this self in here,
> each is reality, complete:
>
> from which arises everything,
> to which all things return again,
> in which all seeming things consist;
>
> which stays the same, unchanged, complete.

However, there are other ways of interpreting this passage, as can be seen by comparing a few available translations. Many of them use the traditional concept of 'brahman': which can be thought of as all-inclusive reality, underlying the creation and appearance of everything in the universe.

In the Ramakrishna Math's publication, *The Bṛhadāraṇyaka Upaniṣad*, 'that' is interpreted as 'Brahman', and 'this' is interpreted as the 'universe'. 'Pūrṇam' is translated as 'infinite'. Accordingly, the passage is taken to describe reality as 'the infinite (Brahman)' from which the universe emanates and into which the universe is assimilated. The resulting translation is:

> That (Brahman) is infinite, this (universe) too is infinite. The infinite (universe) emanates from the infinite (Brahman). Assimilating the infinitude of the infinite (universe), the infinite (Brahman) alone is left.

Swāmī Śarvānanda, in *Īśāvāsyopaniṣad*, translates 'that' as 'the invisible' and 'this' as 'the visible'. 'Pūrṇam' is translated as 'the Infinite'. Accordingly, the passage is taken to describe reality as 'the Infinite': from which the visible universe 'has come out', while the underlying 'Infinite remains the same'. The translation is:

> The invisible is the Infinite, the visible too is the Infinite. From the Infinite, the visible universe of infinite extension has come out. The Infinite remains the same, even though the infinite universe has come out of it.

Swami Prabhavananda and Frederick Manchester, in *The Upanishads*, translate 'that' as 'the things we see not' and 'this' as 'the things we see'. 'Pūrṇam' is translated variously: as 'filled full with Brahman', as just 'Brahman', and as 'all' or 'all that is'. Accordingly, the passage is taken to describe reality as all-filling 'Brahman', out of which 'floweth all that is … yet he is still the same'. The result is a relatively free and stylish translation, as follows:

> Filled full with Brahman are the things we see,
> Filled full with Brahman are the things we see not,
> From out of Brahman floweth all that is:
> From Brahman all – yet he is still the same.

R.C. Zaehner, in *Hindu Scriptures*, translates 'that' as 'beyond', 'this' as 'here', and 'pūrṇam' as 'fullness'. The result is a relatively close, yet stylish translation, as follows:

> Fullness beyond, fullness here:
> Fullness from fullness doth proceed.
> From fullness fullness take away:
> Fullness yet remains.

S. Radhakrishnan, in *The Principal Upanishads*, makes a carefully literal translation and adds a short commentary. In the commentary, 'that' is interpreted as 'transcendent'; 'this' as 'immanent'; and 'pūrṇam' as 'Brahman', whose integrity is unaffected by the created universe.

Translation:

That is full; this is full. The full comes out of the full. Taking the full from the full the full itself remains.

Commentary:

Brahman is both transcendent and immanent.
The birth or the creation of the universe does not in any manner affect the integrity of Brahman.

Swami Sivananda, in *The Principal Upanishads*, also makes a fairly literal translation. But he adds the word 'all' before 'that' and 'this'. And he translates 'pūrṇam' as 'the Whole'. The result is:

The Whole is all That. The Whole is all This. The Whole was born of the Whole. Taking the Whole from the Whole, what remains is the Whole.

Shree Purohit Swami and W.B. Yeats, in *The Ten Principal Upanishads*, make a translation that is both graceful and nearly literal; by leaving 'that' and 'this' as they are, and by translating 'pūrṇam' as 'perfect'. The translation is:

That is perfect. This is perfect. Perfect comes from perfect. Take perfect from perfect, the remainder is perfect.

What do these differing interpretations show? They show at least how one short passage of simple language can throw into question the meaning of concepts like 'this' and 'that', 'full' and 'complete', 'creation' and 'dissolution', 'appearance' and 'reality'.

Consciousness

In the third chapter of the Aitareya Upanishad, an enquiry is made into the nature of self. The conclusion reached is simple. The true nature of self is 'prajnyānam' or 'consciousness'.

In Sanskrit, the word 'jnyānam' means 'knowledge'. Used generally, it refers to all the various different kinds of knowledge: to all our various perceptions, thoughts and feelings, and to all the various expressions and instruments of knowledge that we interpret and use in the world. When the prefix 'pra-' is added, the meaning becomes more specific. In particular, the word 'prajnyānam' refers to 'consciousness': as the illuminating principle of experience, which is shared in common by all forms of knowledge.

The prefix 'pra-' can be interpreted in two ways. On the one hand, it means 'before'; and it thus implies a sense of 'priority': like the English 'pre-', as in 'precede'. On the other hand, it means 'forward' or 'onward'; and it thus implies a sense of ongoing continuity: like the English 'pro-', as in 'proceed'.

In the first sense, where 'pra-' is taken to imply priority, 'prajnyānam' refers to consciousness as the underlying principle of illumination that must exist before any form of knowledge can appear. Consciousness is here described as the underlying *basis* of knowledge: which precedes all the various *forms* of knowledge that appear in our experience.

As experience changes, this underlying principle of consciousness continues, as that which knows the changes. It is always present, at every moment that we know; as the illuminating principle which is shared in common by all the various perceptions, thoughts and feelings that succeed each other in our minds. As different perceptions, thoughts and feelings appear and disappear, consciousness continues through experience, knowing all the changing appearances that come and go.

Thus, in the second sense of the prefix 'pra-', where it is taken to imply ongoing continuity, the word 'prajnyānam' refers to consciousness as the continuing principle of knowledge: which carries on through the changes and variations of experience. Here, consciousness is described as the basis of continuity that enables experience to proceed: as knowledge is passed on from past to future and from person to person.

In short, the word 'prajnyānam' defines consciousness through two essential characteristics: first, its self-evident priority, as the illuminating principle of all experience; and second, its changeless continuity, through all apparent change.

As the Aitareya Upanishad asks what self is, it goes through the various forms of experience that are attributed to a person's self. And then it points out that all these forms of experience are only 'prajnyānasya nāma-dheyāni'. They are only 'attributed names of consciousness'. Or, in other words, they are only apparent attributes which signify the common principle of consciousness underlying them all. By implication, this self-evident and changeless consciousness is the true nature of self, to which the various forms of experience are attributed.

Having thus identified self as consciousness, the Aitareya Upanishad goes on to assert that consciousness is also the true reality of the whole world. This philosophical position is derived in three short statements.

1. *'Prajnyā-netro lokah'*: There is an interesting ambiguity here. The word 'netra' can mean either 'eye' or 'leader'. Accordingly, the statement can mean: 'The world is *seen* by consciousness.' Or it can mean: 'The world is *led* by consciousness.' In the first case, the statement answers the question: how is the world known? Clearly, the world is known by consciousness, which illuminates the appearance of objects in each person's experience. But then, what is the experience by which an object appears? The experience presupposes consciousness, without which there could be no appearance at all. Consciousness comes first, and the appearance of objects can only follow after it. Hence, the argument proceeds to the second meaning indicated above: 'The world is *led* by consciousness.'

2. *'Prajnyā pratishṭha'*: 'Consciousness is the foundation.' This answers the question: if consciousness comes first, then how do objects exist? The existence of each object is established on the basis of consciousness. Whatever object may appear, and however it may appear, consciousness is always there: as an underlying basis of existence that all appearances show. But just such an underlying basis is also described by the word 'reality'. What then is the relationship between 'consciousness' and 'reality'? This question is answered in the third statement.

3. *'Prajnyānam brahma'*: 'Consciousness is all there is.' According to our usual way of thinking about experience, consciousness is that which illuminates each experience, and reality is that which the experience shows. However, even from this description, it is evident that consciousness and reality are always present together, throughout experience. Since both are always present, no person can ever experience one without the other. Though they are thought of differently, they can never be known apart; and so they are

indistinguishable. Two different words are being used to describe the same thing. In truth, consciousness is the underlying reality of each object and of the whole world.

This is the conclusion that is meant to be reached and rigorously tested, by a careful and thorough examination of common experience.

To show how the third chapter of the Aitareya Upanishad might be retold in modern terms, one such retelling is placed alongside a somewhat closer translation below. This is one of the more directly philosophical passages in the Upanishads, and hence it is an example of where a modern retelling could be relatively close to the original text.

Translation (from the Aitareya Upanishad)	**Retelling** (from *FTU*, pages 3-4)
<u>3.1.1</u>	
What is this that we contemplate as 'self'?	What is this self to which we pay such heed?
Which is the self?	
That by which one sees, or that by which one hears, or that by which scents are smelled;	Is it that which sees or hears or senses our perceptions of the world?
or that by which speech is articulated, or that by which taste and tastelessness are known apart?	Does it speak? Does it tell taste from tastelessness?
<u>3.1.2</u>	
That which is this mind and this heart: perception, direction, discernment, consciousness, learning, vision, constancy, thought, consideration, motive, memory,	Or is it mind and heart: which we describe as wisdom, judgement, reason, knowledge, learning, vision, constancy, thought, consideration, motive, memory, imagination, purpose, life, desire, vitality?

imagination, purpose,
life, desire, vitality?

All these are only
attributed names
of consciousness.

These are but names
for consciousness.

<u>3.1.3</u>

This is brahman,
comprehending
all reality.

This is Indra,
chief of gods.

This is the creator,
Lord Prajāpati;

all the gods;

and all these
five great elements
called 'earth', 'air',
'ether', 'waters', 'lights';

and these seeming complexes
of minute things,
and various seeds
of different kinds;
and egg-born creatures
and those born of womb,
and those born
of heat and moisture,
and those born from sprout;

horses, cattle,
humans, elephants,
and whatever living thing,
moving and flying;

and that which stays in place.

Consciousness is everything:
God, all the gods,
the elements of which the world is made,
creatures and things of every kind,
however large or small,
however born or formed,
including all that breathes, walks, flies,
and all that moves or does not move.

All that
is seen, and led,
by consciousness;
and is established
in consciousness.

The world
is seen, and led,
by consciousness.

Consciousness
is the foundation.

Consciousness
is all there is.

All these are known by consciousness,
and take their stand in consciousness.

Coming after consciousness,
the whole world stands in consciousness.

Consciousness is all there is.

3.1.4

By this self,
as consciousness,

he ascended
from this world;

and, attaining all desires
in that place of light,

became deathless,
[that] became.

One who knows self,
as consciousness,
has risen from
this seeming world
to simple truth:

where all desires
are attained
and deathlessness
is realized.

Consciousness and perception

In the Brihadāraṇyaka Upanishad, one story is actually told twice, with much of it repeated word for word, but with a little variation and addition. In this story, Yājnyavalkya distinguishes two different kinds of knowledge.

The first kind of knowledge is called 'vijnyānam' or 'prajnyānam'. 'Vijnyānam' means 'knowing apart', and it refers to the discerning knowledge that knows truth from falsehood. 'Prajnyānam' means 'knowing before', and it refers to the underlying basis of consciousness that must be present before any apparent knowledge can arise.[1]

In one version of the story, Yājnyavalkya describes the self as 'vijnyāna-ghana', which means 'nothing but discerning consciousness'. In the other version, Yājnyavalkya describes the self as 'prajnyāna-ghana', which means 'nothing but underlying consciousness'. In either case, *the true nature of the self is identified with the first kind of knowledge: as pure consciousness, unmixed with anything other than itself.*

Immediately after this, Yājnyavalkya remarks that what appears must disappear; and then he says abruptly: 'Having arrived, there is no knowledge.' But he is now using a different word for knowledge. The word he now uses is 'sanjnyā' (short for 'sanjnyānam'), which means 'knowing with'. This is *the second kind of knowledge: the apparent knowledge of perception, where consciousness appears mixed with perceived objects.* And Yājnyavalkya is saying that *it turns out to be non-existent, once truth has been attained.*

Yājnyavalkya's wife Maitreyī is confused, and tells him so. He replies by distinguishing duality from non-duality.

In duality, one thing is taken to perceive another; and this assumption underlies our apparent knowledge of the world perceived by body, senses and mind.

In non-duality, all that is known is nothing but the knowing self; and this pure consciousness is the true knowledge by which the self illuminates experience. Where such true knowledge has been reached, the apparent knowledge of dualistic perception turns out to be non-existent; because it is a mere appearance that is itself nothing but consciousness.

To attain true knowledge, Yājnyavalkya tells Maitreyī that all she needs is a simple question: 'How can the knower be known?' And with these words,

---

[1]For further discussion, see page 6.

he leaves home; so that Maitreyī is left to go on asking the question for herself.

In what follows, the two original versions are first translated, showing their differing and common passages. Where the two versions differ, their translations are placed side by side. Where they are the same, their common translation is placed in the middle of the page.

After thus comparing the two original versions, another comparison is shown; by reproducing the second version's translation alongside a freer retelling that makes use of both original versions and goes on to a little interpretation and explanation.

One particular problem here is to express the distinction of true and apparent knowledge in modern language. In order to do this:

- The word 'vijnyānam' is translated as 'discerning consciousness' or, more shortly, as 'knowledge' or 'understanding'.

- The word 'prajnyānam' is translated as 'consciousness'.

- The word 'sanjnyā' is translated as 'mixed, perceiving consciousness' or, more shortly, as 'perception'.

- An explanation is interpolated into the retelling, where Yājnyavalkya responds to Maitreyī's confusion about 'sanjnyā' (perception). This interpolation is meant to show, a little more explicitly than the original text, how questions of perception lead on to a consideration of non-dual consciousness.

Translations (from the
Brihadāraṇyaka Upanishad)

<u>2.4.12</u>   <u>4.5.13</u>

'It is as if	'Just as
a lump of salt	the essence
thrown into water	salt itself
were dissolved	has no inside,
into mere water;	has no outside,
'and what there is of it	'but consists
can't be picked out,	entirely
but from wherever taken	of taste alone;
is just salty.	

'So too, dear wife,
this infinite,
unbounded being
is throughout

'nothing else
but pure, discerning
consciousness.

'so too, dear wife,
this self
has no inside,
has no outside,

'but consists
entirely
of nothing else
but consciousness.

'That which has
come together,
rising from
these elements,
vanishes away
along with them.

'Having arrived,
there is no mixed,
perceiving consciousness.

'That's what I say,
dear wife,'
said Yājnyavalkya.

2.4.13

Maitreyī said:

'Just here, dear husband,
you have confused me,
where you say:

'"Having arrived
there is no mixed,
perceiving consciousness."'

4.5.14

Maitreyī said:

'Just here, dear husband,
you have put me
into confusion.

'This I don't
quite understand.'

He said: 'Dear wife,
I am not really saying
anything confusing.

'It is sufficient
for understanding.

         'The self is not
         what vanishes.
         It is by nature
         indivisible
         and indestructible.

<u>2.4.14</u>

'For where duality
seems to arise,

'there one thing smells
something else,

'there one thing sees
something else,

'there one thing hears
something else,

'there one thing speaks
something else,

'there one thing thinks
something else,

'there one thing knows
something else.

<u>4.5.15</u>

'For where duality
seems to arise,

'there one thing sees
something else,

'there one thing smells
something else,

'there one thing tastes
something else,

'there one thing speaks
something else,

'there one thing hears
something else,

'there one thing thinks
something else,

'there one thing touches
something else,

'there one thing knows
something else.

'But, where all of this
has become
the self alone:

'there by what
can what be smelled,

'there by what
can what be seen,

'there by what
can what be heard,

'there by what
can what be seen,

'there by what
can what be smelled,

'there by what
can what be tasted,

'there by what
can what be said,

'there by what
can what be thought,

'there by what
can what be known?

'How can one know
that by which
all this is known?

'Dear wife,
how can
the knower
be known?'

'there by what
can what be said,

'there by what
can what be heard,

'there by what
can what be thought,

'there by what
can what be touched,

'there by what
can what be known?

'This is that self
which is
"not this, not that".

'It is ungraspable,
for it is not grasped.
It is imperishable,
for it does not perish.
It is detached,
for it is not attached.

'Unrestricted,
it is not disturbed
nor suffers harm.

'Dear wife,
how can
the knower
be known?

'You are thus
explicitly instructed,
Maitreyī.

                                          'Just this, dear wife,
                                          is deathlessness.'

                                          Having said this,
                                          Yājnyavalkya
                                          went away.

Translation (from the   **Retelling**
Brihadāraṇyaka Upanishad)   (from *FTU*, pages 97-99)

<u>4.5.13</u>

'Just as   'Salt that is dissolved in water
the essence   cannot be picked out by fingers,
salt itself   can't be held by grasping hands.
has no inside,   It's not a separate lump of salt;
has no outside,   it has no outside nor inside.

'but consists   'But it is there in every drop,
entirely   for each drop tastes of saltiness.
of taste alone;

'so too, dear wife,   'So too, the self is everywhere;
this self   though it can't be picked out by senses,
has no inside,   cannot be conceived by mind.
has no outside,   It's not a bounded piece of world;
                                  it has no outside nor inside.
'but consists
entirely   'But it's here, in all experience,
of nothing else   always here, as consciousness.
but consciousness.

'That which has   'All mind and sense, and all the objects
come together,   they perceive, are formed from changing
rising from   elements; in course of time,
these elements,   they all must change and pass away.
vanishes away
along with them.

'Having arrived,   'Wherever knowledge is attained,
there is no mixed,   no such perception can remain.'
perceiving consciousness.

'That's what I say,
dear wife,'
said Yājnyavalkya.

At this point, Yājnyavalkya paused, with the remark: 'Well, that's what I say.'

<u>4.5.14</u>

Maitreyī said:

'Just here, dear husband,
you have put me
into confusion.
This I don't
quite understand.'

Maitreyī said: 'Just here, I am confused. Where knowledge is attained, how does perception cease? I can't make sense of it.'

He said: 'Dear wife,
I am not really saying
anything confusing.

'The self is not
what vanishes.
It is by nature
indivisible
and indestructible.

Yājnyavalkya replied: 'It isn't really confusing, if you distinguish the changing perception of apparent objects from the continuing basis of consciousness into which each perception is absorbed.

<u>Explanatory interpolation</u>

'As perceptions are absorbed,
they're known as mere appearances
produced by acts of sense and mind
that part reveal and part conceal
the nature of reality.
Thus understood, they are dissolved
in underlying consciousness.

'And consciousness is that which knows
appearances, as mind and sense
perceive a world of changing things.

'But no appearance can exist
apart from knowing consciousness.
Any appearance that departs
from consciousness must disappear
at once, and is no longer there.

'Thus, no appearance has any
existence outside consciousness;
and all of the reality
that each appearance truly shows
is nothing else but consciousness.

'As consciousness illuminates
appearances of seeming world,
in truth, it only knows itself.

'In it, there's no duality
of knowing self and object known.
It is at once the self that knows
and all that's ever really known.

4.5.15

'For where duality
seems to arise,

'there one thing sees
something else,

'there one thing smells
something else,

'there one thing tastes
something else,

'there one thing speaks
something else,

'there one thing hears
something else,

'there one thing thinks
something else,

'there one thing touches
something else,

'there one thing knows
something else.

'Duality seems to arise
where it appears that something sees
or hears or smells or tastes or touches
something else besides itself;

'or where it seems that something
speaks about or thinks about or knows
some object other than itself.

'But, where all of this
has become
the self alone:

'there by what
can what be seen,

'there by what
can what be smelled,

'there by what
can what be tasted,

'there by what
can what be said,

'there by what
can what be heard,

'there by what
can what be thought,

'there by what
can what be touched,

'there by what
can what be known?

'How can one know
that by which
all this is known?

'This is that self
which is
"not this, not that".

'It is ungraspable,
for it is not grasped.
It is imperishable,
for it does not perish.
It is detached,
for it is not attached.

'Unrestricted,
it is not disturbed
nor suffers harm.

'But when all things are realized
as nothing else but self alone,
by whom can what be seen? By whom
can what be heard, smelled, tasted, touched,
described, conceived, desired and known?

'By whom is knowledge truly known?

'The knowing self cannot be any
kind of object in the world.

'Not this, nor that, nor here, nor there
in space or time, it never can
be anything perceived through any
faculty of any body
or of any sense or mind.

'It is unowned, can't be possessed;
it does not die, does not decay,
is unattached, cannot be bound
or limited or qualified;
nor can it ever suffer harm
or be disturbed in any way.

'Dear wife,
how can
the knower
be known?

'Thus, deathlessness may be attained
by asking, till no lies remain:

'*"How can the self that knows be known?"*

'You are thus
explicitly instructed,
Maitreyī.

'Maitreyī, this is the instruction that you
asked. Such is the way to deathlessness.'

'Just this, dear wife,
is deathlessness.'

Having said this,
Yājnyavalkya
went away.

With these words, Yājnyavalkya left home.

Creation

Underlying reality

In the Vedas, the Upanishads and other texts of the Indian tradition, the creation of the perceived universe is described over and over again, in a bewildering variety of different ways that often seem to contradict one another. Given this rich variety of different descriptions, an obvious question arises. Why did the Indian tradition keep trying to describe creation like this, in so many different ways?

Is there some fundamental principle that these various descriptions are trying to describe in common, beneath their apparent differences and contradictions? And is this same fundamental principle also investigated by other descriptions of creation, in other traditions and in modern physical science?

In any description of the world's creation, there is an implicit attempt to do two things. The first is to *expand* the mind's conception: by stretching it back into the past from which the process of creation comes, and stretching it forward to the future where the ongoing process of creation leads.

As conception is thus expanded, there is also an attempt to *deepen* understanding: from the superficial appearance of narrow objects and events, towards underlying principles that continue through apparent differences. This continuity of underlying principle is the unifying basis on which different objects and events are related together. It is therefore implied wherever conception is expanded from limited perceptions of particular objects and events, towards a broader consideration of creation and existence as a whole.

In the Upanishads, the concept of 'brahman' implies both the above aspects: on the one hand, of expanding conception towards the totality of existence; and on the other hand, of deepening understanding towards underlying principle. The word 'brahman' means literally 'growth' or 'expansion' (from the verbal root 'brih' meaning 'to increase'). Its early use in the Vedas is to describe the outpouring of spiritual power in the chanting of sacred words and the performance of sacred rituals. Subsequently, through the mythical conception of creation as a macrocosmic sacrifice, the use of the word 'brahman' developed a more universal sense. As finally used in the Upanishads, it describes on the one hand the entire reality of all creation; and on the other hand, it describes the underlying principle of reality that is always fully present everywhere: in each object and each event, at each locality of space and time.

Thus, the word 'brahman' can be translated as 'complete reality', to which nothing remains to be added by further perception. And it can also be translated as 'the absolute', which is the essence of pure being underlying all appearances produced by the partial perceptions of body, senses and mind.

In all the apparent objects and events that are perceived by body, senses and mind, there is a mixture of superficial appearance and underlying reality. The superficialities of appearance are produced by partial and distorted perception, which must somehow be questioned and corrected, as knowledge proceeds towards truth. By seeing through all such obscuring partialities and distortions, knowledge penetrates towards underlying reality: which is pure being in itself, quite independent of perceived appearances.

One way of approaching this underlying reality is to ask how the perceived universe is created. In particular: from what does creation arise? On what does creation depend? And what becomes of created things as they pass away and lose their manifest identity?

A little reflection will show that the arising of creation is understood in two senses. On the one hand, it is conceived as a temporal process: which arises from a beginning, continues on through time and comes to an end. But, on the other hand, this temporal conception also describes an order of logical priority: where all perceived objects and events arise from an implied and thus logically prior principle of underlying reality.

Whatever objects are perceived to exist, and whatever events are perceived to take place, this implied principle of reality is the basis on which we conceive their creation, their continued existence or occurrence, and their changing and passing away.

In the unmanifest state when nothing appears, before the creation of appearances, this logically prior principle of reality must be there on its own: unmixed with any apparent objects or events. It is also there during the process of creation: underlying all the manifestations of creation, as they take place in the course of time. And it is there on its own once again in the unmanifest state of experience that occurs just after one object of attention has passed out of experience, and before attention turns to some other object.

Both these senses, of temporal process and logical priority, can be seen in the following passage from the Taittirīya Upanishad. Here, the word 'brahman' is translated as 'all reality'.

Translation (from the Taittirīya Upanishad)	**Retelling** (from *FTU*, page 231)

<u>From 3.1</u>

… 'Truly,
that from which
these beings are born,
that by which
born beings live,
that into which
those who depart dissolve,

'that you must
seek to know.

'That is all reality.'…

'The ground from which all things are born,
on which depends all that is born,
and into which all things return,
this ground is what you need to know.

'This ground is all reality.'

Cosmology and experience

If the same principle of complete reality is conceived to be present everywhere, then it must underlie not only the macrocosm of the external universe but also each microcosm of individual experience. Accordingly, the creation of objective phenomena in the external universe and the creation of subjective appearances in individual experience must both finally arise from this same underlying reality.

In the following passage from the Chāndogya Upanishad (3.14.1-4), it is shown that the whole reality of the entire world may be approached subjectively: as the underlying basis from which appearances of perception, thought and feeling arise, in each individual person's experience.

First (in 3.14.1), there is a definition of reality (brahman) as 'tajjalān'. This is a compressed formula which is explained (in the commentary of Shrī Shankara) as made up of the four syllables 'tat', 'ja', 'la' and 'an'. 'Tat' means 'that', and it represents underlying reality. 'Ja' is short for 'janman', meaning 'birth'; 'la' is short for 'laya', meaning 'dissolution'; and 'an' is short for 'ana', meaning 'breathing' or 'living'. Thus, the formula 'tajjalān' may be interpreted to define reality as that which underlies birth, dissolution and living on.

Next, the passage turns to personality; and (in 3.14.2) the self is defined as 'bhārūpa' and 'ākāshātman'. By the description 'bhārūpa' (literally 'that whose form is light'), the true nature of self is identified as consciousness, which illuminates all appearances in each person's experience. In the de-

scription 'ākāshātman', the word 'ākāsha' (meaning 'ether' or 'space' or 'sky')
implies a sense of pervasiveness and continuity through all experience: thus
indicating that the self (ātman) is not a particular body, nor a particular
mind, nor a particular set of senses, nor any conditioned faculty that is limited to a particular personality in some particular locality of space and time.
Taken together, these two descriptions define the self as pure, unconditioned
consciousness at the background of experience: which continues unchanged
through all the changing actions, perceptions, thoughts and feelings of physical, sensual and mental personality.

   Finally (in 3.14.3-4), this changeless self within the heart of each personality is identified as 'all reality' ('brahman'), which includes the entire universe.

Translation (from the Chāndogya Upanishad)	**Retelling** (from *FTU*, pages 104-106)

3.14.1

In truth, all this is complete reality.	In truth, this many seeming world is only one reality,
[It is] that: [in] birth, [in] dissolution, [in] living on.	in which all things seem to be born, seem to live on and pass away.
Thus should the tranquil [mind] reflect [on it].	For those who look, in tranquil peace, where all appearances arise, where all appearances are based, and where they all dissolve again, truth shines in all its clarity.
And further, there is personality, which consists of purpose and intention.	Each personality is made of inclinations, good and bad. Each person's inclinations now build future personality.
As is intention in this world, a person thus becomes: on leaving here becomes.	By choosing to incline this way or that, each one of us builds up what later on our lives will be.

Let him determine
purpose and intention.

<u>3.14.2</u>

Approached
through mind,

embodied by
the breath of life,

appearing in
the forms of light,

conceived as truth,

is the self
at the background
of experience:
continuing
through space and time,

in all actions,
in all desires,
in all odours,
in all tastes,

pervading all
this [world],
unspeaking,
unconcerned.

Through all the changes of our lives,
in every personality,
each one of us experiences
a sense of self, that each calls 'I'.

It is the knowing principle
within our minds, the principle
of life within all living things,
the principle of consciousness
that lights up all appearances.

In all conceptions it is truth:
the background of reality
in all the things we seem to see.

It is the ground on which we stand,
the ground of all created things
we see or hear, conceive or feel.
It is the basis of all sense,
all thought, all sensibility.

Beyond all partial, bounded forms
by which it seems to be expressed,
beyond all troubles of the mind
and body in this seeming world,
self is untroubled, always free.

<u>3.14.3</u>

This is my self
within the heart,
tinier than a grain
of rice or barley,

or than a mustard seed,
or than a millet grain,
or than the kernel
of a millet grain.

This self within each person's heart ...

is smaller than the smallest thing
that eyes can see or mind conceive ...

This is my self   is greater than the whole wide earth
within the heart,   beneath our feet; is greater than
greater than the earth,   the sky's expanse above our heads,

greater than air and sky,   than any far-flung universe
greater than heaven,   that instruments can show to us,
greater than these worlds.   than all the complex, subtle worlds
                               imagination can conceive.

3.14.4

In all actions,   In truth, this self within each heart
in all desires,   is absolute reality:
in all odours,   found everywhere, in everything,
in all tastes,   beyond all things that seem to be.

pervading all   Where outside things have been perceived
this [world],   through body's senses or through mind,
unspeaking,   perception introduces doubt
unconcerned,   that mind or body may be wrong.

this is my self   But where the world's appearances
within the heart;   are left behind and self is found,
                               there self directly knows itself.
this is all reality.

'In it,   It *knows* because it *is* itself,
leaving here [from   and thus no room remains for doubt.
world's appearances],
I am come to unity.'   Whoever realizes self
                               knows finally, beyond all doubt,
For one who   unbounded, deathless certainty.
can say this truly,
there is no doubt.

Thus said Shāṇḍilya.

[Thus said] Shāṇḍilya.

Creation from self

   If each person's true self is identical with complete reality, then it must be
possible to understand this inner core of self as the underlying source of all
creation. Such an approach is described in the Brihadāraṇyaka Upanishad,
2.1.20.

Translation (from the Brihadāraṇyaka Upanishad)	**Retelling** (from *FTU*, page 65)

<u>2.1.20</u>

'As a spider issues forth with thread, 'as from fire little sparks come forth;	'As a spider from its body sends out threads and weaves a web, or as small sparks come forth from fire;
'so too, from this self are issued forth all living energies, all worlds, all gods, all created beings.	'so too, from this same self come forth all energies, all lives, all worlds, all gods and all created things.
'Of that, the final teaching is said to be "the truth of truth".	'This is that final teaching which is said to be the "truth of truth".
'[Beneath appearances or seeming world], living energies are truth. Of them, this is the truth.'	*'Truth is all things; and of all things, self is the truth of each.'*

The seed of creation

Each person's body, senses and mind are only a very small part of a much larger universe. How then could anyone find, within this little personality, a self which is all the reality that underlies the entire vastness of the perceived universe? An answer is given in the Chāndogya Upanishad, 6.12.1-3: where the apparent immensity of the entire universe is conceived to rise from inner self just as a great tree may arise from the unseen essence of fertility within a tiny seed.

In the retelling reproduced below, the original passage is modified by adding a short interpolation that introduces the concept of consciousness, in order to make the meaning a little clearer and more specific for a modern reader. Though this concept of consciousness does not occur directly in the original passage, it is indirectly implied by the word 'aṇiman': which occurs three times. The direct meaning of 'aṇiman' is 'minuteness' or 'subtlety', but it comes from the verbal root 'aṇ', meaning 'to sound' or 'to breathe' or 'to live'. As this derivation shows, the word does not refer only to minuteness of physical size, but also to subtlety of meaning and life and spirit. It may be of interest to note here that the Sanskrit roots 'aṇ' and 'an' are cognate with the Latin 'anima', meaning 'soul' or 'spirit', and 'animus', meaning 'mind' or 'thinking principle'.

Translation (from the Chāndogya Upanishad)	**Retelling** (from *FTU*, page 114)

6.12.1

'Bring a fruit from this nyagrodha tree.'	Then, Shvetaketu's father led him to a spreading banyan tree, whose fruits had fallen on the ground.
'Here, Sir.'	
'Break it.'	'Pick up a fruit…. Break it open…. Tell me what you see.' 'Tiny seeds.'
'It is broken, Sir.'	
'What do you see in it?'	
'These seeds, Sir, like tiny particles.'	
'Well, break one of them.'	'Break one of these…. What do you see?'
'It is broken, Sir.'	'Nothing. The seeds are much too small.'
'What do you see in it?'	
'Nothing at all, Sir.'	

6.12.2

[Shvetaketu's father] said to him:	'And yet, within each tiny seed, there is a subtle something which your eyes don't see, something unseen from which this spreading tree has grown.
'Truly, dear son, this minuteness which you do not see,	
'truly, dear son, of this minuteness the great nyagrodha tree thus stands.	

'Be sure of this, dear son.

<u>Explanatory interpolation</u>

'So too, from unmixed consciousness,
which mind and senses can't perceive,
arises this great-seeming world.

<u>From 6.12.3</u>

'That which is
this minuteness
is that "this-itself"-ness
which is all this [world].

'Pure consciousness, the essence of
each mind and heart, is all the world's
reality. That is the truth.
That is what you really are.'

'That is truth.
That is self.

'Shvetaketu,
you are that.'…

Light from the seed

The following passage from the Chāndogya Upanishad (3.17.7) shows
further the intimate and subtle connection that was conceived in the Upanishads between consciousness and the primal seed of creation.

Translation (from the
Chāndogya Upanishad)

Retelling
(from *FTU*, page 107)

<u>3.17.7</u>

Looking up
from darkness,
we perceive
all around
our own higher light,

Self is the ancient, timeless seed
from which all life and world are born.
Through all that seems obscurity,
self shines undimmed as consciousness,
the light that lights all other lights.

coming from
the primal seed.

That light is self, and self alone.

And we have gone
to the sun:
the higher god
among the gods,

the highest light,
the highest light.

The basis of experience

In the following passage from the Muṇḍaka Upanishad (1.1.3-9), an enquiry is made into the underlying basis of all experience. And the conclusion reached (in 1.1.9) is that this underlying basis is consciousness, from which arises all apparent existence of name, form and matter.

Here, the retelling has been derived by adding in an explanatory introduction, and by elaborating the compressed ideas of the original passage with a fair degree of interpretation and explanation.

* The introduction is meant to explain the concept of reality that is implied by Shaunaka's somewhat cryptic question: 'What is it that being known, all this becomes known?'

* The rest of the retelling elaborates ideas in a way that somewhat modifies the original passage. In particular, the concept of consciousness is brought in rather earlier than in the original, where consciousness is explicitly described only at the end (in 1.1.9): by the three phrases 'sarvajnyah' (translated below as 'that which knows in all experience'), 'sarvavid' (translated below as 'that which knows all that is known') and 'yasya jnyānamayam tapah' (translated below as that 'whose intensity consists of knowledge').

Translation (from the Muṇḍaka Upanishad)	**Retelling** (from *FTU*, pages 184-188)

Explanatory introduction added into retelling

The great householder Shaunaka
was blessed with an enquiring mind,
unsatisfied by partial truth.

He thought: 'In this vast universe,
there are so many different things
our minds and senses seem to see.

'In each perception we perceive,
so little of the world seems shown.

'As mind and sense perceive the world
they show us small appearances,
which change from changing points of view.

'A mountain seen from far seems small;
from closer up it grows in size.

'A person on the lower slopes
sees grass and trees, hears rustling leaves,
smells flowers, feels the warmth of sun;

'but higher up stark cliffs appear,
with craggy shapes of barren rock,
and eerie sounds of rushing wind,
and scentless feel of chilly air.

'And yet, these different seeming things
are varying appearances
through which one mountain can be known.

'So too, in all experience,
the many things we seem to see
are differing appearances
through which we know one universe.

'What is this one same universe
in which our minds and senses see
so many different seeming things?

'Is there some way to understand
this one complete reality
we know through all appearances
of everything that seems to be?'

1.1.3

The great householder
Shaunaka duly
approached Angiras,
and asked:

So Shaunaka, with due respect,
approached the teacher Angiras
and asked: 'Can knowledge of the world's
reality be so complete
that all the many things we seem
to see are understood in it?

'Sir, what is it
that being known
all this
[apparent universe]
becomes known?'

'Can something so complete be found
that knowing it knows everything?'

1.1.4-5

To Shaunaka,
Angiras said:

'Those who know
complete reality
say that there are two
kinds of knowledge
to be known:

'The truth you seek,' said Angiras,
'is plain to see, and can be found
by anyone who wishes it.

'To know it you must go beyond
all scriptures, sciences and arts:
for these are mere constructions, made
by partial body, sense and mind.

'the higher
and the lower.

'Among the lower
of these are:

'Beneath all learned structures, built
of form and name and quality,
upon what basis do we join
the partial views of sense and mind,
to make our knowledge more complete?

'the Rig Veda,
the Yajur Veda,
the Sāma Veda,
the Atharva Veda,

'phonetics, ritual,
grammar, etymology,
metrics, astrology.

'This basis must be firm. It must
remain: while mind and body change,
and changing views give rise to sights,
sensations, feelings, thoughts that come
and go in our experience.

'And the higher
is that by which
the unchanging
is attained.

1.1.6

'That which can't
be seen or grasped,

'It is no object seen by mind
and sense; for all such objects come
into experience when they
are seen, and go away again
as our attention turns elsewhere.

'Unseen by sense, unseen by mind,
it is the knowing basis which
must carry on, continuing
through changing sense and changing mind,
as seeming objects come and go.

'It is not body, sense or mind,
for these are merely instruments
of change and action in the world.

'It is no object that can act
on other objects; nor can it
be acted on, by anything.

'which has
no family, no class,
no eyes or ears,
no hands or feet,

'It has no family, nor class;
nor has it eyes that see, nor ears
that hear, nor hands that touch or hold,
nor feet that stand or walk or run.

'It does not act; it only knows.

'It is pure consciousness: which lights
up all appearances that come
and go in our experience.

'which is constant
and continual

'in different
happenings,

'All space, all time, all difference,
all change are known by consciousness.
Thus space and time and difference
and change cannot apply to it.

'It is the undivided base
from which divided space is known,
the unity in difference,
the changeless continuity
which knows all change and passing time.

'extending everywhere,

'It's always here, in every one
of us, each moment that we know;

'whatever we may seem to know,
whatever it may seem we do
not know, or only know in part.

'Upon this base of consciousness,
all objects are perceived and thus
are manifested in the world.

'In consciousness, all seeming things
arise, exist and come to end.

'completely subtle;

'that is the changeless
source of being
which the wise
and steadfast see.

'Beneath gross things of outer sense,
beneath all subtleties of mind,
it is creation's changeless source:

'from which all seeming things come forth,
on which each seeming thing depends,
to which each thing returns again.

1.1.7

'As a spider
issues [thread]
and takes [it] in,

'as plants grow
on the earth,

'as hair from
a living person's
head and body;

'so too, from
the unchanging,
everything arises here.

'As from a spider thread comes forth
and is drawn in, or just as plants
grow out of earth and when they die
dissolve in earth again; so too
all things that we perceive, throughout
the manifested universe,

'arise from changeless consciousness,
are manifest as consciousness
taking on apparent form,
and when they end are shown dissolved
as nothing else but consciousness.

1.1.8-9

'Through
purposeful intensity,
reality becomes
constructed

'[as a seeming
universe
made up
of seeming things].

'Each moment of experience,
a person's mind and sense perceive
a partial view that seems to show
some object in the universe.

'At different times, through different minds,
through different capabilities
of sense, we seem to see a vast
variety of different things.

'And thus it seems that we perceive
a universe of vast extent,
containing more complexity
than sense or mind can comprehend.

'From that
food is born.

'In this vast-seeming universe,
our little senses only see
small objects, each a little piece
of matter formed in space and time.

'From food,
living energy,

'When objects interact, we see
the energy that they exchange;
and thus material things seem formed
of subtle energy that flows,
through space and time, to manifest
the outward world our senses see.

'If outward things are seen as forms
of manifesting energy,
then what is thus made manifest?

'What do forms mean? How can they be
interpreted, to understand
more than our senses seem to see?

'mind,
truth;

'Forms are interpreted by mind:
which is expressed in forms,
and which reflects within itself
to ask for truth that forms express.

'worlds,
and in actions
the deathless.

'Where mind turns back towards its source,
it is dissolved in consciousness;
which has no parts, nor suffers change.

'That which knows
in all experience,

'There, partiality and change
do not apply; and thus complete,
undying truth is realized.

'and which knows
all that is known,

'But where the mind is turned towards
an outer world of seeming things,

'whose intensity
consists of knowledge;

there only partial truths are seen,
expressed by mind in outward acts....'

'from that is born
all this
[apparent] existence:
name, form and food....'

Creation through personality

In an extended passage from the Brihadāraṇyaka Upanishad (1.4), creation is described as arising, from underlying self, through personality. This passage has two aspects: mythical and philosophical.

The mythical aspect describes creation as an event that took place in the far distant past, at the beginning of time. Here, the universe is mythically conceived to have arisen from an absolute self which existed on its own before the creation of time; and which continues to exist unchanged, underlying the apparent universe, as created time proceeds.

The philosophical aspect uses this creation myth to explain and investigate experience, as it is known in the present. Here, each person's experience is described as arising from a common, underlying principle of self: which is to be identified through the statement 'aham brahmāsmi' ('I am the absolute' or 'I am complete reality').

In the following translation and retelling (as elsewhere in this book), it is the philosophical aspect that has been emphasized. The translation is fairly literal, but it omits some sections of the original that are too elaborately mythological. And where a word or phrase may be translated in differing ways, the more philosophical alternative has been chosen. In particular, the word 'agre' (which occurs several times in the original passage) has been translated as 'first and foremost', instead of the more usual and more mythological translation 'in the beginning'.

In the retelling, the philosophical aspect is further emphasized, by replacing the past tense of mythical imagination with a present tense of philosophical reflection. Thus, the mythological parts of the original have been modified, through a replacement of mythical metaphor by philosophical interpretation.

Translation (from the Brihadāraṇyaka Upanishad)	**Retelling** (from *FTU*, pages 44-50)

<u>1.4.1</u>

First and foremost, self alone was this:	Right from the start, each person's self is common, plain humanity:

which is established
as purusha
[the common,
underlying principle
of 'human-ness'
in every person].

which different-seeming persons share
through changing times and changing minds
in different personalities.

He looked, and saw
nothing else but self.

Whatever sights a person sees,
whatever may appear to mind,
in all of our experiences,
the self is always present there.

Thus nothing ever is perceived
without the presence of the self.
And nothing anyone perceives
can ever be apart from self.

He first declared:
'I am.'

Thus, he came
to be called 'I'.

And therefore even now,
one who is addressed
says first just 'It is I';

and then speaks
another name,
which becomes his.

First and foremost, every person
starts by thinking: 'This is I.'
And so each person is called 'I'.

When asked for one's identity,
what first response comes up at once,
spontaneously, from deep within?

One first identifies oneself as 'I',
and only then come other names
by which one is identified.

He who came first,
before all this,
burned up all ills.

Therefore he is purusha
[plain, simple
'human-ness'].

One who knows thus,
truly burns up
that which seeks
to come before
this ['human-ness'].

This, which comes first, before all things,
burns up all misery and wrong.
Anything that tries to push
in front of plain humanity
burns up, for one who knows just this.

1.4.2

He was afraid.
Therefore, a person
who is lonely
feels afraid.

But people seem to have known fear:
a lonely person feels afraid.

He himself made
this observation:

When such a person, all alone,
observes 'Of what am I afraid,
if there is nothing else but I?';
then with this thought fear vanishes.

'Since there is
nothing else but me,
of what then
am I afraid?'

From that alone
his fear departed.

For, of what
should one be afraid?
It's only from
a second thing
that fear arises.

Without a second thing to fear,
what is there to be frightened of?

1.4.3

But still,
he was not pleased.
Therefore,
a lonely person
is not pleased.

And people also seem to feel
unhappiness: a lonely person
suffers want of warmth and joy.

He desired a second.
He became the size
of a woman and man
in close embrace.

By longing for companionship,
life in this world has taken shape
as male and female intertwined.

This very self
he caused to fall
divided into two.

The self has thus been made to seem
divided, fallen into two,
as male and female have been formed:
each one an uncompleted half.

From that,
husband and wife
came into being.

Therefore, this
[personality]
is a half-fragment
of oneself.

This is just what
Yājnyavalkya truly said.

Therefore, this space
is just filled
by a woman.

With her,
he came together.
From that,
human beings were born.

Each one then suffers emptiness,
which must be filled by someone else.
So male and female join in one,
and from this match we all are born.

1.4.5

He knew:
'I myself am creation;
for I created all this.'

The knowing self in each of us
is underlying consciousness
from which appearances arise
in everyone's experience.

Hence
he became
creation.

Since everything comes out of it,
it's that which seems to have become
this many seeming universe.
It's all creation in itself.

One who knows thus
comes to be
at this very creation
of his.

To know it is to stand as self,
which one has truly always been,
at all creation's timeless source.

1.4.7

That itself was this,
at that time unmanifest.

The world we see is only this:
which is itself unmanifest.

That, by mere
name and form,
was manifested:

Only by name and form has this
seemed to be manifest, as world.

[conceived] as
something
with that name
or with this form.

That is this, even now,
by mere name and form
made manifest:

The world seems manifested when
some seeming name is used for this,
some seeming form is seen in this.

[conceived] as
something
with that name
or with this form.

He is this, pervading
here [in the body],
up to the tip
of [a person's] nails:

This is that common principle
which permeates the universe
into each corner of the world;

just as a blade is placed
within its sheath,
or as all-sustaining [fire]
in its all-sustaining web.

just as a blade fits in its sheath,
or as the energy which forms
the universe lies there within
all matter that is formed by it.

Him they do not perceive,
for [as perceived]
he is incomplete.

This universal principle
cannot be known through force or power
of life's intentions, nor through speech,
nor sight, nor hearing, nor through mind.

Merely breathing,
he gets to be
called 'breath';

speaking, [he is
called] 'speech';
seeing, [he is]
'sense of sight';

hearing, [he is]
'sense of sound';
thinking, [he is
called] 'mind'.

These are only
names of functions
of his.

These are merely names of functions:
each of which is incomplete.

Whoever thus pays heed
to each, one by one,
does not know;

for thus [appearing]
through each [function],
one by one,
this [appearance]
becomes incomplete.

One should heed him
only as that
which is called 'self';
for, in it, all these
[appearances] turn out
to be one.

That is this,
to be attained:
that which is this self
of all of this.

For, by this [self],
one knows all this.

Just as [a tracker
finds] by footprints,
one may find.

Who knows this
finds praise and poetry.

Looking through such partial functions,
all that's seen is incomplete.

Such means can never quite know truth.

Reflecting on the self alone,
all partial functions merge in one.
In all the world that we perceive,
this self is what we need to reach:
for everything is known by this.

True honour, glory, grace, success
arise unasked for one who knows
all things as signs of only this.

1.4.8

That is this,
dearer than a son,
dearer than wealth
and property,

dearer than all else,
deepest within,
that which is this self.

Beyond all else, it is the self
that's near and dear: more than all wealth,
more than all friends and family.

Of him who speaks
of something other
than the self as dear,
one may say:

'He will lose
what he holds dear';
for it may
very well be so.

One should heed
only the self as dear.

For one who heeds
only the self as dear,
that which is dear
is indestructible.

When anything besides this self
is thought an object of desire,
then desire turns to torment:
even desire for God himself.

In any object of desire,
self is all we wish to find.

Where self is truly seen in love,
there love is found to be complete,
for what is loved can never end.

1.4.9

It is said:

'Given that men think
of becoming everything
through knowledge
of the absolute;

'what did it know,
that absolute,
from which it
became everything?'

By knowledge of the absolute,
a person hopes to be complete.

This absolute we thus invoke,
what does it know, as it creates
from its own self the world we see?

1.4.10

First and foremost,
this [universe]
was the absolute itself.

It knew itself:
'I am the absolute.'

From that, it became
everything.

The absolute is only this,
which first and foremost knows itself.

It knows: '*I am the absolute.*'

And on this base appear from it
the many things we seem to see.

Among the gods,
whoever recognized it
became it.

So also among seers.
So also among men.

Seeing that
in truth as this,
the seer Vāmadeva
reflected: 'I am Manu
[first of men].
I am the sun.'

That is this, even now.
One who thus knows,
'I am the absolute',
becomes all this.

Even the gods themselves
have not the power
for his undoing;
for he becomes their self.

But one who heeds
an alien deity, thinking
'That is different,
I am different';
he does not know.

He is like
a mere beast
of the gods.

Just as many beasts
may serve a man,
thus each man
serves the gods.

If just one beast
is led astray,
it is not liked.
What then, of many?

Whoever realizes this,
and knows 'I am the absolute',
becomes complete in everything.

The gods themselves cannot undo
one who has found identity
with that which is their very self.

But if one heeds an alien god
who seems apart from one's own self,
truth can't be known; for then one is
a beast of burden to the gods.

As beasts of burden have their masters,
so do people have their gods.

It is not liked when any beast
is taken from its master's fold.
Nor is it liked when someone finds
this truth: that in each one of us
the self is absolute, and free.

Therefore, it is not liked
by these [gods] that men
should know this [self].

<u>1.4.15</u>

That is this:

It is this absolute that seems
to have evolved, through course of time,
as knowledge, power, enterprise
and service, in society.

the brāhmaṇa
[the man of knowledge],

the kshatriya
[the man of power],

the vaishya
[the man of commerce]

the shūdra
[the man of service].

That, through fire alone
has come to be:
the [sacred] absolute
[worshipped] in the gods,
the man of knowledge
among men.

[That] through power
[has come to be]
the man of power;
through commerce,
the man of commerce;
through service,
the man of service.

Therefore,
people seek the world:
through fire alone
among the gods,
in the man of knowledge
among men.

We dream of gods to seek out worlds
of sublimated energy;
and in our waking life we seek
out knowledge of our universe.

For, by these two forms,
the absolute
has become [manifest].

For energy and learning are
both forms in which the absolute
has been expressed in what we see.

But, whoever
leaves this world,
without seeing
his own place;
[for him it is] unknown.

He does not take
possession of it, just like
the Vedas not recited
or other work not done.

Whoever, here,
not knowing thus,
does work
even of great value;

that same [achievement]
of his, in the end,
must be exhausted.

Blindness to our own existence
robs our lives of all reward;
every one of our achievements
must in time dissolve away.

The self alone
should be heeded
as [all] the world.

One who heeds
the self alone
as all the world,
his achievement
is never exhausted.

But, if one only sees the self
absolute in all existence,
life's reward can never die.

For, from this same self
is created
whatever is desired.

Everything that is desired
is produced from this same self.

1.4.16

In truth, this self
is the world
of all beings.

The world of beings is this self.

It, through that
which worships
and sacrifices,
is the world of gods.

It is the mythic world of gods
created by religious rite.

Likewise, through that
which recites, [it is]
the visionaries' [world].

It is the fancied world of thought
created by an author's words.

And, through that
which offers to ancestors
and desires progeny,
[it is] the
ancestors' [world].

It is the world tradition makes
respecting past experience
and also seeking something new.

And, through that
which shelters humans
and nourishes them,
[it is the world]
of human beings.

It is the world we humans make
from need for home and sustenance.

And, through that
which obtains
for animals
grass and water, [it is
the world] of animals.

It is the world of animals,
where grass and water must be found.

Through that on which,
in homes of this,
wild beasts and birds
[and other creatures]
even to the ants
subsist, [it is]
their world.

It is the earth on which subsist
beasts, birds and other forms of life,
in bodies that are homes of this.

As one may wish
no harm of one's
own world, so too
all creatures wish
no harm, to one
who knows thus.

One should wish well of one's own world.
At heart, all beings do wish well,
seen in that light which knows just this.

That, in truth, is
what is known,
what is sought
to be known.

Whatever anyone has known,
whatever anyone has sought
to know, is nothing else but this.

<u>1.4.17</u>

First and foremost,
self alone was this,
one alone.

In truth, there is one single self,
with nothing else at all besides.

He desired: 'May there
be a wife for me.
And, may I
have progeny.
And, may there
be wealth for me.
And, may I do
[my] work.'

And yet, it seems that people seek
out company of other selves,
that people feel desire for birth
and property and gainful work.

Just this much is desire.
Not even one
who wishes to
can find [by wishing]
more than this.

Such limited desires can't
grow to be more than limited,
not even if one wants them to.

Therefore, even now,
a lonely person desires:

A lonely person wants to find
companionship, wants a new life,
wants things and looks for work to do.

'May there be
a wife for me.
And, may I
have progeny.
And, may there
be wealth for me.
And, may I do
[my] work.'

So far as he
does not obtain
any one of these,
to that extent he feels
merely incomplete.

And where such wishes aren't fulfilled,
a person does not feel complete.

But, [examined] further,
completeness is his.

How can a person be complete?

[Pure consciousness
of] mind alone
is his self.

Speech is the wife
[that brings forth
his progeny].

Sight is [his]
human wealth,
for by sight he knows it.

Hearing is his
divine wealth,
for by hearing he hears it.

Self alone is his work,
for by the self
he does work.

He is this:
fivefold sacrifice,
fivefold animal,
fivefold 'human-ness'.

Fivefold is this:
all this whatsoever.
That is this.

Who knows thus
attains everything.

Through consciousness that's known as self;
through speech that's married to the self;
through purpose as its progeny.

Through property that, known by sight,
is known as nothing else but sight;
through worth that, known by sense, is known
as only sensibility.

Through work that shows true purity
of self, on which all life depends.

In all the multiplicity
of actions, persons, creatures, things,
throughout this many-seeming world,
the self is one and one alone.

All is reached, by knowing this.

Waking from deep sleep

How do we experience the creation of the perceived world from inner
self? An answer is given in the following passage from the Kaushītaki Upanishad (4.19-20). Here, deep sleep is understood as a state of pure consciousness, unmixed with any appearances of an outside world. Hence, on waking
from deep sleep, a person experiences a creation of the apparent world,
through waking mind and senses, from underlying consciousness.

This underlying consciousness is the true nature of self. It shines by itself
in deep sleep; and it continues unchanged through the dream and waking
states: as the ultimate, illuminating basis of all appearances in the dream
and waking worlds.

Translation (from the Kaushitaki Upanishad)

Retelling (from *FTU*, pages 159-161)

From 4.19

… In depth of sleep
no dreams are seen.

In depth of sleep, no mind appears
conceiving different seeming things;

and mind's attention does not direct
living energy from consciousness
to different seeming objects
in some world that mind conceives.

Thus here, in dreamless sleep, all
outward-seeming energies of life
have been withdrawn, and differences
are all dissolved in consciousness:
which shines alone, by its own light,
unmixed with any seeming thing.

4.20

Then, in this very
living breath,
oneness is attained.

Into that
which is this:

goes speech
together with all words,

goes seeing
together with all sights,

goes hearing
together with all sounds,

goes mind
together with
all thoughts.

Here, every day, unnoticed in
the simple peace of dreamless sleep,
all life attains to unity
of underlying consciousness,
from which all lives and minds arise.

Whenever someone falls asleep,
attention is drawn in: from world
of waking sense, through dreaming mind,
to unconditioned consciousness,
which shines unmixed in depth of sleep.

All speech, all words and all they mean,
all seeing, hearing, sights and sounds,
and all perceptions, thoughts and feelings
then dissolve: absorbed again
into their underlying base
of consciousness, from which they rise.

When one awakes,

just as from burning fire
sparks come forth
in all directions,

so too, from this self,
living breaths come forth
each to its place;

from living breaths,
the senses;
from the senses, worlds.

But, when a person wakes from sleep,
outgoing energies of life
appear, through various faculties
of mind and personality.

As sparks come forth from blazing fire,
so too from consciousness come forth
the various energies of life
that mind and personality
disperse through their activities.

From these activities arise
appearances of mind and sense;
and thus, from these appearances,
the worlds that we perceive are born.

This living breath in itself
is the self
of consciousness:

which has pervaded
this [seeming] self
of body, right to
the hairs and nails.

Just as a razor
is contained
within its sheath,

or as the all-sustaining
[fire] in its
all-sustaining web;

so too, this self
of consciousness
has pervaded
the [seeming] self
of body, right to
the hairs and nails.

Beneath appearances of world
perceived by senses and by mind,
consciousness continues on
through every moment of experience:

lighting all appearances
that rise in dream or waking state;

and shining self-illuminated,
on its own, in depth of sleep.

It is each person's real self:
the inner principle of life
that is expressed in every act
of mind and body in the world.

That is this self,
on which these
[seeming] selves depend:

All seeming selves, of body or
of sense or mind, depend upon
this real self of consciousness.

as on a chief, his own
[followers depend].

Just as a chief makes use
of his own [followers];

or, as to a chief
his own [followers]
are of use;

so too, this self
of consciousness
experiences [the world]
through these selves;

and even so,
these selves
are in service
to this self.

Indeed, as long as Indra
[chief of gods] did not
understand this self,
demons overcame him.

But when he understood,
he struck down and
conquered the demons:

attaining pre-eminence,
independence and
sovereignty of all gods
and all beings.

So too,
one who knows thus
strikes down all ills

and attains pre-eminence,
independence and
sovereignty
of all beings;

one who knows thus,
one who knows thus.

Just as a chief is represented
by his followers, who act
with his support and for his sake;

so too, the real self is
represented by the seeming selves
of body, sense and mind: whose actions
all depend on its support
and are, unknowingly or
knowingly, done only for its sake.

On consciousness, the real self,
these seeming selves always depend
for all they do or seek to do.

But it does not depend on them;
for it is there in depth of sleep,
when seeming selves have all dissolved.

As long as this true self is not
correctly understood and known,
a person's actions are not firmly
anchored in the changeless ground
from which they come, on which they stand
and where they find all that they seek.

Thus, if this ground of self remains
unknown, poor body, sense and mind
keep being overcome by their
own demons of uncertainty
and partiality and ill.

But one who knows the truth of self
has reached that certain, deathless ground
of unconditioned consciousness:

where ills have all been overcome
and freedom has, at last, been won.

The creation of appearances

Appearances are not created only at the moment of waking from deep sleep. They go on being created at every moment of waking and dreaming experience. Thus, each person's experience can be viewed as a stream of changing appearances: created by the perceptions, thoughts and feelings which come and go in that person's mind. As the mind perceives and thinks and feels, it creates the succession of changing appearances that rise up from underlying consciousness, in each person's experience.

Where modern physical cosmology is almost entirely focused upon the objective world, traditional cosmologies had a more pronounced subjective aspect. Before the development of modern telescopes and space exploration, traditional cosmology was used more for metaphorical reflection than for experimental astrophysics. In the Upanishads at least, the purpose of cosmology is clear. It is to meditate and reflect, upon the underlying reality from which the manifest universe is created.

For someone who meditates or reflects, the physical creation of the universe is not of course at hand; for it has taken place over an enormous period of time, stretching back to very remote events in the far distant past. However, what is at hand are the appearances of perception, thought and feeling: rising up and being created from underlying consciousness.

In effect, this is an immediate, mental creation of the world's appearances, as they are manifested in an individual's experience. Through the correspondence that was conceived between the macrocosm of the external universe and the microcosm of individual experience, traditional descriptions of cosmic creation can often be interpreted as metaphors for the creation of appearances from underlying consciousness.

In what follows, an attempt is made to interpret the Nāsadīya hymn from the Rig Veda (10.129) in just this way. First, to give a reader some sense of the original text, a translation by A. A. Macdonell is reproduced.[1] Then, one way is shown as to how the text might be further interpreted and retold, by placing a somewhat extended retelling alongside the appropriate lines (or parts of lines) from Macdonell's translation.

---

[1]From *A Sourcebook in Indian Philosophy*, edited by Sarvepalli Radhakrishnan and Charles A. Moore, Princeton University Press, Princeton, 5th paperback printing, 1973.

Hymn of creation
Rig Veda 10.129 – Macdonell's translation

Non-being then existed not nor being:
There was no air, nor sky that is beyond it.
What was concealed? Wherein? In whose protection?
And was there deep, unfathomable water?   *1*

Death then existed not nor life immortal;
Of neither night nor day was any token.
By its inherent force the One breathed windless:
No other thing than that beyond existed.   *2*

Darkness there was at first by darkness hidden;
Without distinctive marks, this all was water.
That which, becoming, by the void was covered,
That One by force of heat came into being.   *3*

Desire entered the One in the beginning:
It was the earliest seed, of thought the product.
The sages searching in their hearts with wisdom,
Found out the bond of being in non-being.   *4*

Their ray extended light across the darkness:
But was the One above or was it under?
Creative force was there, and fertile power:
Below was energy, above was impulse.   *5*

Who knows for certain? Who shall here declare it?
Whence was it born, and whence came this creation?
The gods were born after this world's creation:
Then who can know from whence it has arisen?   *6*

None knoweth whence creation has arisen;
And whether he has or has not produced it:
He who surveys it in the highest heaven,
He only knows, or haply he may know not.   *7*

<table>
<tr><td>Macdonell's Translation
(of the Rig Veda 10.129)</td><td>Retelling
(from *FTU*, pages 270-274)</td></tr>
</table>

<u>1.</u>

Non-being then existed not nor being:	Before conception has appeared, no absence can arise at all; for objects have not been conceived that may be 'there' or be 'not there'.
There was no air, nor sky that is beyond it.	Nor yet can qualities arise, nor overarching principles pervading different-seeming things; for these too have not been conceived.
What was concealed?…	What is the base of consciousness from which conception must arise, before the world can be conceived? Unmixed with seeming, doubtful things that rise from mind's uncertainties, what does pure consciousness contain?
… Wherein?…	Where can such consciousness be found?
… In whose protection?	Whose is this unmixed consciousness? How does its knowledge carry on, as things appear and disappear, conceived by doubtful, changing mind? Just what provides stability, security and certainty, as consciousness continues on: through seeming things that come and go, appearing when they are perceived and disappearing when they're not?

And was there
deep,
unfathomable
water?

Through changing mind's apparent waves
of form and name and quality,

what really is the consciousness
of which each seeming wave consists,
just like the boundless depths below?

2.

Death then existed not
nor life immortal;

Before conception rises up
from unconditioned consciousness,
there is no change nor difference;
for time and space aren't yet conceived.

With nothing born, there is no death
and so there can't be deathlessness.

Of neither night
nor day
was any token.

Since world has not yet been conceived,
there's nothing that appears by day
or disappears again at night.

No world appears as we awake,
nor disappears when we're asleep.

There is no night. There is no day.
There is no waking state, nor sleep.

By its inherent force
the One
breathed windless:

Within the world that mind conceives,
our bodies live by breathing air.
So too, our minds breathe meaning out
through words and acts, and breathe back in
perceptions from an outer world.

But consciousness is life itself,
which lives by its inherent light
that lights itself, without the need
for any breathing out or in.

No other thing
than that
beyond existed.

In truth, as known by consciousness,
what seems outside is known within.

There really is no outside world
that's separate from some inner mind.
There's no outside and no inside.

<u>3.</u>

Darkness there was at first by darkness hidden;	When mind looks down to its own depths from where conception seems to rise, a blinding darkness first appears concealed in its own ignorance.
Without distinctive marks, this all was water.	Here, all seems primal, inchoate: with unseen powers surging up from depths of dark obscurity.
That which, becoming, by the void was covered,	From this uncertain, shifting base, whatever truth may be conceived comes dressed in empty vanity:
That One by force of heat came into being.	of mind that's driven blindly on by energies and powers of will it doesn't fully understand.

<u>4.</u> [2]

Desire entered the One in the beginning:	Desire turns on consciousness right from the start of seeming life:
It was the earliest seed, of thought the product.	where mind is seeded by desire to form a stream of changing thoughts by which the world is then conceived.

[2]Stanza 4 can be translated alternatively (and fairly literally) as follows:

> First of all, upon that [One]
> desire has turned entirely.
> This has been mind's primal seed.
> Searching heart with mind intent,
> men of vision, in non-being,
> have found out the bond of being.

The main difference is at the start. (a) 'Agre' is translated by Macdonell as 'in the beginning', but here above as 'first of all'. (b) 'Samavartatādhi' is translated by Macdonell as 'entered', but here above in the more elaborate and literal sense of 'turned entirely upon' ('turned' from 'avartata', 'entirely' from 'sam', and 'upon' from 'adhi').

The sages searching
in their hearts
with wisdom,

Found out the bond
of being
in non-being.

When thought turns back to heart within,
to clarify obscurities
and search for undistorted truth,

at first there seems blank nothingness
where everything has disappeared.

What is this seeming nothingness?

It is the absence of apparent
things, not of reality.

In it, all seeming thought dissolves
and what remains is consciousness,
unmixed with any seeming thing.

As thought dissolves, pure consciousness
shines out as all reality:

where different-seeming things are joined
as mere appearances of one.

5.

Their ray
extended light
across the darkness:

Unseen by body, sense or mind,
the light of consciousness extends
through all the universe it shows:

through everything that seems to be
or not to be, through space and time,
through every state of changing mind.

Where mind completely disappears,
as in the peace of dreamless sleep,
there comes a state that mind conceives
as dark and empty nothingness.

But nothingness cannot seem dark
unless it's known by consciousness:
whose light shines unconditioned here,
unseen by body, sense and mind.

But was the One
above or
was it under?

Back in the world that mind conceives,
just where can consciousness be found?

Is it beneath appearances?
Is it above what mind desires?

Creative force
was there,
and fertile power:

Is it the subtle seeds of mind
from which creation is conceived?
Is it the energies and powers
that shape the world and get things done?

Below was energy,
above was impulse.

Is it the underlying power
that moves creation from the start?
Is it the drive that follows on
to look for better life beyond?

6.

Who knows for certain?
Who shall here
declare it?

Who really knows? Just what is it
in each of us that knows the things
our minds conceive and senses see?

Whence was it born,
and whence came
this creation?

Just who or what in us can tell
from where appearances are born,
from where creation is conceived?

The gods were born
after this
world's creation:

Our faculties of mind and sense
are part of the created world.
They cannot therefore come before
this world has been conceived by mind.

Then who can know
from whence
it has arisen?

What then is prior to the mind?

Just who or what in us can know
from where conception rises up
to form the world we think we see?

7. [3]

None knoweth whence creation has arisen;	From where does seeming world arise?
	Does it in truth arise at all, or does it only seem to rise from incorrect appearances mistakenly perceived by mind?
And whether he has or has not produced it:	
He who surveys it in the highest heaven,	The changing things of seeming world, and their conception in our minds, are known by changeless consciousness: which carries on, while seeming things and mind's conceptions come and go.
	In everyone's experience, as feelings, thoughts, perceptions and their seeming objects come and go,
	pure consciousness alone remains: continuing through time and change, to know all these appearances.
He only knows, or haply he may know not.	It's only from this final base, of unconditioned consciousness, that world's conception can be known; if it is truly known at all.

---

[3]Stanza 7 can be translated alternatively (and fairly literally) as follows:

> From where has this creation come to be?
> Has it been established or has it not?
> Only its witness in the highest heaven
> truly knows [it] or knows if [it is] not.

The main difference is in the last line. 'Yadi' has been translated by Macdonell as 'haply' (i.e. 'perhaps'), but here above as 'if'. Macdonell's translation thus expresses a sense of doubt about all knowledge of the created world. This alternative translation goes on to suggest an enquiry into pure, unconditioned consciousness: whose self-illuminating knowledge continues independent of whether the created world seems to exist or not.

Change and continuity

Movement

In the first chapter of the Chāndogya Upanishad, there is a short passage (1.9.1) which asks about the nature of movement. And the answer is given that movement is really nothing but space; because all beings arise from space, come to end in space and are contained in space.

How is this passage to be interpreted? In the original Sanskrit, the word used for 'movement' is 'gati', and the word used for 'space' is 'ākāsha'.

Let us first consider the Sanskrit word 'gati'. In general, the word means 'going' or 'moving' (as an abstract noun derived from the verbal root 'gam', meaning 'to go' or 'to move'). Based on this general meaning, the word 'gati' is used in many particular ways. In the sense of 'going *from*' or 'issuing', it can be used to mean 'origin' or 'source' or 'basis' or 'essence'. In the sense of 'going *between*' or 'proceeding', it can be used to mean 'process' or 'means' or 'path' or 'way' or 'state'. In the sense of 'going *to*' or 'reaching', it can be used to mean 'goal' or 'end' or 'refuge' or 'resort'.

Accordingly, the above passage (Chāndogya Upanishad 1.9.1) can be translated in rather different ways.

S. Radhakrishnan interprets 'gati' as 'goal', in the following translation (from *The Principal Upaniṣads*):

> 'What is the goal of this world?' He replied, 'Space, for all these creatures are produced from space. They return back into space. For space is greater than these. Space is the final goal.'

Juan Mascaró interprets 'gati' as 'origin' or 'source', as implied in the following translation (from *The Upanishads*):

> Wherefrom do all these worlds come? They come from space. All beings arise from space, and into space they return: space is indeed their beginning, and space is their final end.

Swāmi Swāhānanda (in *The Chāndogya Upaniṣad*) interprets 'gati' as 'essence':

'What is the essence of this world?' 'Ākāśa,' said (Pravāhaṇa); 'all these beings arise from Ākāśa alone and are finally dissolved into Ākāśa; because Ākāśa alone is greater than all these and Ākāśa is the support at all times.'

And further, by interpreting 'gati' more simply and directly as 'going' or 'movement', the same passage could also be translated:

> 'What is the movement of this world?'
> 'It is space,' he said. 'All these beings
> rise produced from space alone
> and, given up, return to space.
> For space is greater than they are.
> Space is what carries on, beyond.'

This last translation is a little elaborated in the retelling reproduced below (from *FTU*, page 101):

> What is this change and movement
> that appears to form our world?
>
> All seeming motion is but space;
> for everything is formed in space.
> When formed, each thing is part of space;
> whatever moves, must move in space.
> Contained in space, all forms arise
> and move and change and pass away.
>
> All moving things and changing forms
> arise, take shape, continue on
> and come to end in space alone.

The continuing background

What is the meaning of the Sanskrit word 'ākāsha', which has been translated above as 'space'?

The word 'ākāsha' can also be translated as 'ether' or 'sky'. Its translation as 'ether' shows that it refers to the *continuity* of space. As 'ether', 'ākāsha' was taken to be an all-pervasive substance which is present everywhere, unconfined and unlimited by the boundaries of any locality in space or time.

This 'ether' is not a gross material substance which is somehow separated into pieces, so as to form the bounded objects that our limited senses perceive. It is too subtle to be perceived by any of the senses, because they are all limited instruments whose range of perception is always confined within the boundaries of particular localities. Unseen by the senses, the 'ether' is known only by its continuity: as the continuing background of space and time, in which each particular object is located.

Accordingly, the word 'ākāsha' does not refer to 'space' in the narrow sense: as distance and locality, which *separate* particular objects. In Sanskrit, when space is conceived in this narrow sense, it is described by the words 'dik' (literally 'direction', 'quarter') and 'desha' (literally 'place', 'region'). By contrast, the word 'ākāsha' conceives of 'space' in a much broader and more universal sense: as *continuing* space and time, which together contain the entire universe and which thus *connect* different objects. In this conception, all of space and time are taken together: as the pervasive and unifying background of the world, in which each physical and mental thing must be located.

This is why the word 'ākāsha' is also used to mean 'sky'. For the sky was taken to be a continuing, universal background: overarching all particular things on earth. Accordingly, it was a cosmic symbol for the continuing background of experience that enables particular objects to be contrasted or compared, and hence to be distinguished apart or related together.

There is a striking correspondence here with modern physics. At the end of the nineteenth century, light was thought to travel as a wave motion in a highly pervasive material medium called 'ether'. This 'ether' somehow pervaded other substances like glass and water and air: thus enabling light to be transmitted through them. But it was much more rarefied than other substances, because it somehow filled empty space: thus enabling light to be transmitted through a vacuum tube from which the air has been pumped out; and enabling light to be transmitted from the sun and the stars to the earth, though the vast empty spaces that are seen in the sky.

In the early part of the twentieth century, Albert Einstein put forward the theory of relativity: which thinks of light as transmitted by the innate properties of space and time. In this theory, the transmission of light and other phenomena, such as gravity, are conceived to manifest the underlying 'geometry' of space and time. This 'space-time geometry' is simply the way in which apparently different events are connected together, in a 'space-time continuum'.

Here, light is no longer thought to be transmitted through a material medium that must be added on to space and time, as something extra to them. Instead, light is transmitted, and other phenomena are manifested, by the 'space-time continuum' itself. The so-called 'ether' is nothing else but the continuity of space and time.

This new way of looking at the 'ether' went along with a broader and more fundamental change in the way that physicists conceive the world. The theory of relativity does not think about the world as a mechanical system of pieces of matter that are extraneously added on to space and time. Instead, it has been developing a conception of the entire physical universe as a 'space-time continuum': where space, time, matter and energy are essentially inter-related and must be considered together; in order to understand an invariant and continuing reality beneath the variations and changes of relative appearance.

In much the same way, though generalizing their approach to consider mental as well as physical experience, the Upanishads conceive of 'ākāsha' as the background continuity of space and time; and they enquire into an unchanging reality that underlies this continuity.

In the following translation and retelling of a passage from the Brihadāraṇyaka Upanishad (3.8.3-11), the word 'ākāsha' is translated as 'ether'.

Translation (from the Brihadāraṇyaka Upanishad)

Retelling (from *FTU*, pages 74-76)

<u>3.8.3</u>

She said: 'Yājnyavalkya,

'that which is above heaven,

'that which is below earth,

'that which is between these two, heaven and earth;

'that which was, and is, and is to be;

'that which is thus spoken of, in what is that woven, warp and woof?'

'Yājnyavalkya ... What is the substance of all that is said to be existence: above heaven, below earth, in earth and heaven and in between, in all that was and is and is to be?'

3.8.4

He said: 'Gārgī,

'that which is
above heaven,

'that which is
below earth,

'that which is
between these two,
heaven and earth;

'that which was, and is,
and is to be;

'that which is
thus spoken of,
is woven,
warp and woof,
in ether.'

'This all-pervasive substance is called "ether". It is not a gross substance, like "earth", which can be fashioned into separate objects, as a potter fashions clay into pots. Instead, this "ether" is the highly subtle substance of underlying continuity: which enables each object or event to be understood, in relation to other objects and events located elsewhere in space and time.

'Through the limited perceptions of body, senses and mind, limited objects and events appear at the forefront of attention. Each particular object or event is thus a limited and partial appearance of a much larger world. Each such limited appearance, of only one particular object or event, is understood in relation to a background of experience which somehow comprehends other objects and events that are not explicitly seen or thought of at the time.

'As attention turns from one appearance to another, the background of experience continues, enabling different appearances and different objects and events to be related. In every object or event that appears in experience, this continuing background is understood. Its continuity thus extends throughout experience: through all space and time, through all relationships and through all causes and effects.

'The subtle substance "ether" is essentially unmanifest. Unlike gross matter, it is not manifested by its separation into different objects and events. Instead, it underlies experience, as the continuing background that is implicitly understood in the perception of all objects and events. It is the continuing background of the entire world: the complete background of all-containing space, time and causality.'

<u>From 3.8.5 and 3.8.7</u>

She said: 'Salutation
to you, Yājnyavalkya,
who have answered this
[first question] of mine.
Hold ready for the other....

'In what indeed is ether
woven, warp and woof?'

'Yes, this is a satisfying answer, and it leads to my second question. On what basis does this continuing background pervade all of existence?'

<u>3.8.8</u>

He said: 'Gārgī,
those who know reality
describe it as
the changeless.

'The basis of all space, all time,
all cause, cannot itself be changed,
nor qualified, by changing
qualities of space and time and cause.
Thus, it is described as "changeless".

'Not gross, nor fine,
not short, nor long,

'not flaming red,
nor syrupy,

'not shade,
nor darkness,
not air, nor ether;

'not connected,
without taste or smell,
without eyes and ears
or speech or mind;

'not sharp,
it has no vital force
or face or measure,
no inside, no outside.

'It does not
consume anything.
Nothing consumes it.

'It is not coarse, nor yet refined;
it is not long or short, nor wet
or dry; nor has it colour,
shade or darkness, taste or smell.

'It is not "air", nor "ether":
for it has no qualities,
and it cannot be related
to anything besides itself.

'It has no eyes, no ears, no speech,
no mind; it is not sharp, nor has
it vital force, nor face, nor measure.
Nor does it consume, nor is consumed.
It has no outside, nor inside.

3.8.9

'Under the guidance
of this same
changeless principle,
Gārgī, the sun and moon
are kept in place.

'Under the guidance
of this same
changeless principle,
Gārgī, heaven and earth
are kept in place.

'Under the guidance
of this same
changeless principle,
Gārgī, moments, hours,
days and nights,

'fortnights, months,
seasons, years
are kept in place.

'Under the guidance
of this same
changeless principle,
Gārgī, rivers flow
'from white mountains,

'some eastwards,
some westwards,
each in its own direction.

'Under the guidance
of this same
changeless principle,
Gārgī, people praise
those who give;

'the gods are connected
with the sacrificer,
the ancestors with
the darvī offering.

'Based on this changeless principle,
the sun and moon are kept on course,
and heaven and earth remain in place.

'Moments pass in due succession,
days give way to nights and nights to days,
seasons alternate and years pass by.
Rivers rise and flow from mountains.
People work to seek reward.

<u>3.8.10</u>

'Gārgī, whoever
does not know this
changeless principle,

'Wherever there is ignorance
of this one changeless principle,
work but results in passing gain.

'but in this world
makes offerings
and sacrifices,

'and intensifies
self-discipline,
thousands of years;

'for such a person
that [achievement]
is merely passing.

'Gārgī, whoever
leaves this world
in ignorance of this
changeless principle
is an object of pity.

'To leave the world in ignorance
of changeless truth is misery.

'But Gārgī, one who
leaves the world
with knowledge of this
changeless principle
realizes everything.

'But one who knows this changeless truth
has reached the goal of all desire,
and leaves the world in deathless peace
with nothing further to attain.

<u>3.8.11</u>

'This, Gārgī, is that same
changeless principle
which is not seen,
but is the see-er;

'This changeless principle
cannot be seen:
it is the see-er.

'which is not heard,
but is the hearer;

'It can't be heard:
it is the hearer.

'which is not thought,
but is the thinker;

'It can't be thought:
it is the thinker.

'which is not known,
but is the knower.

'It can't be known:
it is the knower.

'Other than this,   'Nothing else can see or hear
there is no see-er.   or think or feel or understand.

'Other than this,
there is no hearer.

'Other than this,
there is no thinker.

'Other than this,   'Nothing else can know at all.
there is no knower.

'Gārgī, in this very   'Gārgī, this changeless, knowing principle is
changeless principle,   the basis on which stands the all-pervading
the ether is woven,   continuity called "ether". This is the ultimate
warp and woof.'   basis of all apparent existence.'

Objective and subjective

Towards the end of the preceding passage, there is a significant change of approach: from objective to subjective. Where Yājnyavalkya has been describing a changeless principle that underlies all the changes of the perceived world, he suddenly reverses the direction of attention, from that which is known to that which knows: 'This same ... changeless principle ... is not seen, but is the see-er; ... is not known , but is the knower.' (3.8.11)

In the following translation and retelling from the Chāndogya Upanishad, 3.18.1, the distinction of objective and subjective approaches is made explicit. Here, the word 'ākāsha' is translated as 'the overarching space of sky'.

Translation (from the   **Retelling**
Chāndogya Upanishad)   (from *FTU*, page 108)

<u>3.18.1</u>

Mind may be   Subjectively, the thinking
meditated on   principle may be considered
as all reality: all reality, all that there is.
this with regard
to inner self.

Next, with regard
to gods above:
the overarching
space of sky
as all reality.

And then objectively, the background
of the world, continuing
through all appearances in space
and time, may be considered all
there is, all true reality.

These two are advised:
with regard
to inner self,
and with regard
to gods above.

Both of these meditations are
advised: the first subjectively,
the second one objectively.

Unchanging self

What is the subjective approach, which enquires into the nature of 'the knower' or the 'inner self'?

In the following translation and retelling of excerpted passages from the Brihadāraṇyaka Upanishad, chapter 4, self is described as the illuminating principle of consciousness: which continues unchanged through all the apparent changes of each person's experience. Here, 'ākāsha' is translated as 'space' or as 'the background of space'.

Translation (from the
Brihadāraṇyaka Upanishad)

Retelling
(from *FTU*, pages 83-93)

<u>4.3.7</u>

'Which is the self?'

'But then, what is this knowing self?'

'That which is this,
whose nature is
consciousness
in living functions,

'It is the light of consciousness
within each living creature's heart.

'the light within the heart,
purusha [the principle
of personality].

'Being the same,
it journeys through
both worlds,

'And though it seems to journey through
a waking world of outside things
or inner worlds of dreaming mind,

'seeming to think
and move.

'For, sleeping,
it transcends the world,
the forms of death.

'in truth, it always stays the same
through all appearances of change.

'In depth of sleep, the self is shown
beyond all worlds of changing form.

4.3.8

'It, this same purusha,
being born,
assuming a body,
is projected
mixed with ills.

'Departing, dying,
it gives up ills.

'Where this self seems born as body,
it seems to suffer body's ills.
Each body dies, all ills must pass;
that which remains, unchanged, is self.

4.3.9

'Of that indeed,
of this purusha,
there are two states:

'this and
the other-worldly state.

'At the junction
is the third:

'the state of sleep.

'There are two seeming states of self:

'as body in an outside world;

'or mind, conceiving subtle worlds
made up of its own thoughts and dreams.

'But, joining these apparent states,
is that third state where seeming stops,
where thoughts and dreams have all dissolved
and no appearances remain.

'This is the state of dreamless sleep;
the timeless state that is achieved
when meditation stills the mind;
the state between successive thoughts,
where previous thought has come to end
and further thought has not begun.

'Here, in this unconditioned state,
self shines unmixed with alien things
that make it seem what it is not.

'Standing at that
joining state,
it sees these two:

'this and
the other-worldly state.

'Now, whatever is the way
to the other-worldly state,
when that way is taken
both ills and joys are seen.

'When it goes to sleep,
it takes back
the measure of this
all-containing world.

'Having itself destroyed,
having itself created,
by its own radiance,
by its own light,
it sleeps.

'Here, this purusha
itself is light.

'Remaining always in this state
of unconditioned purity,
self lights the body's waking world
and worlds of mind that dreaming brings.

'Whatever state seems to appear,
all seeming ills and seeming joys
are lit and known by self alone.

'As mind withdraws from world in sleep,
the whole created world dissolves
in all creation's shining source:
where self is light which lights itself.

4.3.10

'In that, there are
no chariots, nor those
in harness to chariots,
nor roads;

'but it projects
chariots, and those
in harness, and roads.

'In that, there are
no joys, no pleasures,
no delights;

'but it projects
joys, pleasures
and delights.

'Here, where all dreams dissolve in light
from which they come, there is no change,
nor cause of change, nor place for change.
There is no need for fancy's flight,
there are no bounds, there is no pain.

'In that, there are
no pools of water,
no lotus ponds,
no flowing streams;

'but it projects
pools, lotus ponds
and streams.

'For, it is the creator.

4.3.11

'[On] that,
there are these verses:

'"By sleep annihilating
bodily existence,

'"this that does not sleep
looks out
on sleeping things.

'"And, taking light
back in again,
it comes to [its] place:
[this] golden purusha,
sole swan [one spirit
in all things].

'When body sleeps, the body's world
dissolves in unmixed consciousness;
as body's seeming consciousness
returns again to its true source
in that unsleeping, deathless self
which knows all worlds, all dreams, all sleep.

4.3.12

'"Guarding the
inferior nest [the body]
by living breath,
it journeys on undying,
beyond, outside the nest;

'"and [thus]
goes deathless
where desire [wills]:

'"[this] golden purusha,
sole swan [one spirit
in all things]...."

'The body's seeming life is bound
to breath, to circulating blood,
to many other vital needs
that keep our bodies functioning.

'But self is free, it has no needs;
it is untouched by seeming change.
As life itself, it cannot die.

'Through passing states of wakefulness
and dream and sleep, the self alone
goes on from state to state, unchanged.

<u>From 4.3.15-17</u>

'That is just this,
in this pure serenity.

'Enjoying itself
and moving,

'merely seeing
good and ill,

'it runs back in reverse,
back to source:
for sleep itself.

'There, whatever it sees,
it is not followed by that;
for this purusha
is unattached....

'That is just this,
in this sleep.

'Enjoying itself
and moving,

'merely seeing
good and ill,

'it runs back in reverse,
back to source:
for the very end of waking.

'There, whatever it sees,
it is not followed by that;
for this purusha
is unattached....

'That is just this,
in this end of waking.

'Enjoying itself
and moving,

'merely seeing
good and ill,

'In sleep, in dreams, in wakefulness,
the self is always free: unchanged
by all the good and evil things
that seem to pass before its light.

'It only knows, it does not act;
and so it cannot be attached.

'it runs back in reverse,
back to source:
for the very end of sleep.

4.4.16

'That in front of which
the year revolves
together with its days;

'to that
the gods pay heed:

'the light of lights,
the lasting principle
of deathless life.

'Before the self, all moments pass,
each day proceeds and turns to night,
each season gives way to the next,
and seasons cycle into years.

'For self is knowing consciousness,
which knows all time, all place, all things.
It is the ever-present light
that lights all lights in all we know.

4.4.17

'That in which
the five groups of five
and the background
of space
are established;

'by thinking of self
as that alone,

'one who [thus] knows
the deathless absolute
is deathless.

'Through all appearances that come
and go in our experience,
this knowing consciousness goes on
from difference to difference,
from change to change. And through all change
it is the vital core of life,
which lasts, as all else comes and goes.

'This never-changing consciousness
is that immortal absolute
upon which all experience rests.
Just knowing it brings deathlessness.

4.4.18

'Those who have known
the breath of breath,
the eye of eye,
the ear of ear,
the mind of mind;

'they have realized
the ancient,
primordial
absolute.

'It is the living principle
in all the various lives we lead.
It is the seeing principle
in all the various sights we see.
It is the hearing principle
in all appearances of sound.

'It is the knowing principle
in all our minds' experiences:
in all the meanings we perceive,
in all the various thoughts we think,
in all the feelings that we feel.

4.4.19

'Through mind alone
to be perceived,

'in it there's no
diversity at all.

'Whoever seems to see
diversity in it,
goes on from death
to death.

'But, in this knowing principle,
which knows all change and difference,
no change or difference exists.

'Whoever sees diversity
and change sees but appearances,
which only lead from death to death.

4.4.20-21

'As one alone
to be perceived, it is
immeasurable,
permanent.

'Stainless,
beyond all space,
the unborn self
is great and permanent.

'Recognizing that alone,
a steadfast realist
should work
for knowledge.

'Let there not be
[mere] thought
of many words;
for that
is weariness of speech.

'Self is that one unchanging truth
which can't be known by changing mind.

'Shared in common by all difference,
stainless through all imperfection,
never born in all creation,
limitless through space and time;
beyond all words, beyond all thought,
beyond all forms and qualities;

'self is known by simply being,
because its nature is to shine.

<u>From 4.4.22</u>

'This is that same   'True self is unborn consciousness,
great unborn self,   the ground of all experience,
whose nature is   from which appearances are born.
this consciousness
in living functions.   'It is life in living function,
                                 source and aim of all intention,
'In this space   untouched depth of all emotion,
within the heart,   infinite, within each heart.
it rests:
the controller of all,
the lord and ruler
of everything.

'It is not increased   'No action can affect this self:
by work well done,   good actions cannot make it grow,
nor diminished   bad actions cannot cause it loss.
by work ill done: It is complete reality,
                                 beyond all partial-seeming things.
'this lord of all,
this ruler of beings,
this protector of beings.

'This is the bridge   'It is the underlying ground
that holds apart,   from which all difference seems to rise,
for the separation   on which all different things seem to
and the joining   exist apart, to which all
of these worlds....'   seeming difference must return again....'

Continuity

Towards the end of the preceding translation (4.4.22), the self is said to rest 'in this space within the heart': where the word 'space' again translates the Sanskrit 'ākāsha'. What is this 'space within the heart'?

As described earlier (pages 61-64), when 'ākāsha' is conceived objectively, it refers to 'space' as the continuing background which relates together the differing and changing objects that we perceive in the outside world. Thus, when 'ākāsha' is conceived subjectively, as 'within the heart', it evidently describes a corresponding background of 'inner' experience. More simply put, it is the background of consciousness: which continues through experience, while perceptions, thoughts and feelings come and go.

But then, what is the relationship between this background of subjective experience and the background of the world? Ultimately, in each person's experience, everything in the world is known subjectively. Each object is experienced through perception, thought and feeling. As the background of consciousness continues through perceptions, thoughts and feelings, it also continues through all experience of the world. It is thus the continuing background not only of subjective experience, but also of the entire world.

Such a reconciliation of subjective and objective approaches is described in the following translation and retelling of excerpted passages from the Chāndogya Upanishad, 8.1-4. Here, the Sanskrit word 'ākāsha' is once again translated as 'space' (in 8.1.1,3).

This translation and retelling may be taken as an instance where a rather cryptic and condensed original has been retold by supplementing it with a considerable degree of interpretation, explanation and elaboration. In particular, the retelling includes an explanatory introduction which does not correspond directly to any passage in the original.

Translation (from the Chāndogya Upanishad)	**Retelling** (from *FTU*, pages 121-125)

<u>Explanatory introduction added into retelling</u>

Our bodies, senses and our minds
keep changing in a changing world.
And so, whatever they perceive
is by its nature changeable.

But, as this change keeps going on,
how is it known that things have changed?
How can something be compared
with what it was before it changed?

Where variation is perceived,
what is it that knows the change
of passing states which come and go?

It must be there before the change,
to know the state that was before.
And it must still be there when change
has taken place, to know what has
become of what was there before.

> Wherever there is variation,
> that which knows must carry on
> through changing states that come and go.
>
> Each state gives way to other states,
> but that which knows the change remains.
>
> This knowing principle remains
> unchanged, unvarying: through all
> the change and all the variations
> body, sense and mind perceive.
>
> Whatever is perceived must vary;
> that which knows is never changed.
>
> As body, sense and mind perceive,
> appearances of world are formed.
> And all of these appearances
> are known by light of consciousness.
>
> Perception isn't that which knows;
> it only forms appearances
> through changing body, sense and mind.
>
> That which knows is consciousness;
> it lights up all appearances.
> It's always there, throughout experience,
> always shines by its own light.
>
> Perception changes every moment;
> consciousness remains unchanged.

From 8.1.1 [1]

Om. Assuredly,   At the surface of our minds,
in this stronghold   things appear and disappear:

---

[1]In 8.1.1 and 8.1.4, the phrase, 'this stronghold of the absolute', refers to personality (i.e. body, senses and mind): in the sense that personality is the apparent 'stronghold' of consciousness, which is in truth the absolute. A little later, in 8.1.5, it is shown that the real 'stronghold of the absolute' is not perishable personality, but the changeless self (which is pure consciousness, unmixed with body, senses and mind). See page 95 and following, for further discussion about these concepts of personality and the impersonal principle that lives within.

of the absolute,

that which is this
subtle lotus flower
is a home.

In it is
a subtle
inner space....

as attention is directed
from one object to the next.

Beneath this stream of changing show,
different things must be related
at the background of experience,
where each thing is understood.

As mind's outer surface changes,
consciousness continues on,
putting different things together
at the depth of understanding:
changeless background of experience,
inner basis of the mind.

From 8.1.3

... Just as great as
the space [of all
the world] is this inner
space within the heart.

This unchanging consciousness,
which shines within each mind and heart,
has neither magnitude nor form.

In itself,
contained within, are
both heaven and earth,
both fire and air,
both sun and moon,
lightning and the stars.

And yet, we find contained in it
everything we seem to see:
all the entire universe
of earth and sun and moon and stars,
all space, all time, all worlds, all minds.

Whatever of this is
and whatever is not,
all that is
contained in it.

From 8.1.4 [2]

... If,
in this stronghold
of the absolute,

If all existence is thus found
within each person's mind and heart,
what happens when a person dies?

[2]See footnote 1, just above.

is contained all this,
all beings and all desires;

then what remains of this   Can all of being be destroyed,
when old age comes to it   when some poor mind in little body
or when it is destroyed?   suffers harm and passes on?

<u>From 8.1.5</u> [3]

... By the ageing   In truth, as mind and body seem
of this [body],   to suffer harm and die, such harm
it does not age.   and death are mere appearances,
                                     which cannot rise or stand except
By the killing   as they are known by consciousness.
of this [body],
it is not killed.

It is the truth,   But consciousness illuminates
the [real] stronghold   itself; it shines by its own light.
of the absolute.   It does not rise or pass away.

In it,
desires are contained.

It is the self: It is the self, within us all,
                                     whose nature is to light itself,
free of evils,   and thus to light appearances
free of old age,   which are themselves but consciousness.
free from death,   True self, as unmixed consciousness,
free from grief,   depends on nothing else at all.
free of hunger   It is untouched by seeming change
and thirst;   or seeming harm or seeming death.

desiring truth,
thinking truth....

<u>8.4.1</u>

Assuredly,   Self is the continuity
that which is self   that lives unchanged through change; it is
                                     the bridge that joins all differences.
is the bridge
and boundary

[3]See footnote 1, just above.

that separates
and joins these worlds.

And yet, it also is the basis
of discrimination, by which
different things are told apart.

No night or day,
nor age, nor death,
nor grief,
nor good action,
nor bad action,

When understanding passes from
appearance to reality,
no day or night, no height or depth,
no age, nor death, nor fear, nor grief,
nor good or bad can pass to self;

crosses over
onto this bridge.

All ills turn back from it;
for it is free of evils,
this place of the absolute.

for no conditioned quality
of seeming world applies to it.

8.4.2

Truly therefore,
crossing over
to this bridge,

the blind becomes
not blind,
the wounded becomes
not wounded,
the afflicted becomes
not afflicted.

As truth of self is realized,
all blindness is removed from sight,
all wounds are healed, all pain dissolves,
all bonds are loosed, all lack is filled;

Truly therefore,
crossing over
to this bridge,
even night turns out
to be just day,

and darkness shines as dazzling light
of unconditioned consciousness.

for it is fully well
illuminated, this place of
the absolute.

Life

Energy

In the Upanishads, as in so much of traditional thought, life was often conceived through the metaphor of 'living breath'. This metaphor is expressed in the Sanskrit word 'prāṇa'. Literally, 'prāṇa' means 'breathing forth' or 'breathing onward'. But it also carries a more metaphorical sense of meaning: as 'life' or 'living spirit' or 'the breath of life'.

In this sense, life was conceived as a kind of subtle energy: which animates the living actions of our bodies and minds, and which similarly animates the actions of other living creatures that we perceive in the world around us.

Moreover, all movements in the entire universe were conceived to act together, in a single living 'macrocosm'. Just as each living creature is motivated by its own energy of individual life; so too the entire universe was conceived to be animated by a universal living energy, expressed in everything that happens everywhere.

In Sanskrit, the perceived universe is commonly described by the word 'jagat': which is the present participle of the common verb 'gam', meaning 'to go' or 'to move'. Thus 'jagat' quite simply means 'moving'; and when it is used to describe the world as a whole, it implies a totality of perceived movements manifesting the universal energy that underlies them all. This conception is described in the following translation and retelling from the Kaṭha Upanishad, 6.2. Here, the word 'prāṇa' is translated as 'living energy'; and the word 'jagat' is translated as the 'changing universe'.

Translation (from the Kaṭha Upanishad)	**Retelling** (from *FTU*, page 35)
<u>6.2</u>	
That which is all this changing universe, whatever has come forth, is living energy.	The whole created universe is made of living energy that moves and oscillates and shines.

It moves and oscillates
and shines:

a great terror, an uplifted thunderbolt.	This boundless store of restless cosmic energy has terrible destructive power. It's like an upraised thunderbolt: to petty ego's fragile life, identified with little body, sense and mind.
They who know this become deathless.	But if, transcending petty ego, all the world is known as life – as only living energy – then how can death arise at all?
	For one who knows the world like this, as only life, there is no death. In truth, there's only deathlessness.

Expression

Modern developments in physics, in particular in relativity and quantum field theory, have made us familiar with the idea of a changing universe made up of underlying energy. But what is meant by describing this energy as 'living'?

Basically, movements and actions are called 'living' when they are implied to express some sort of underlying consciousness. And then, we do not understand these movements and actions merely by looking out to external objects that act upon one another. In addition, we reflect back into our own experience, in order to understand the underlying consciousness that is expressed in living behaviour.

By contrast with the objective energy that is described and manipulated through the calculations of physical science, living energy is understood by subjective reflection: as expressing an underlying consciousness that is shared in common by observer and observed.

Such reflective understanding is most obvious in our knowledge of human beings and other living creatures; but it is also an essential, though more subtle component in our knowledge of the world as a whole. For, in order to put our fragmentary knowledge together, objective calculations are insufficient in themselves. They depend upon underlying principles of order and meaning, which we somehow understand in them. And this understanding requires a subjective reflection into our own consciousness, where underlying principles are found shared in common with the external world.

However we put together knowledge of the world, and however we conceive of its functioning as a whole, our knowledge is based upon subjective principles of order and meaning from our own consciousness.

Thus, both for living creatures and for the world as a whole, there are two different levels of consideration. First, they may be considered objectively: as made up of objects or objective parts that act upon one another. And second, they may be considered subjectively: as expressing consciousness. In the first case, they are treated as mere instruments or objects of action, external to life. In the second case, they are treated as 'living' or 'alive'.

This rather delicate question of expression is raised in the Prashna Upanishad, 3.3, which says that life ('prāṇa') appears in the body as a shadow-image ('chāyā') produced from inner self by the activity of mind:

ātmana esha prāṇo jāyate	From self, this life is born.
yathaishā purushe	Just as this on purusha
chāy-	is a [mere] shadow-image;
aitasminn	[so too] upon this [self],
etad ātatam	this that is drawn out
manokriten-	by mind's activity
āyāty asmin charīre	comes into this body.

The literal translation above is meant to show two particular problems that arise when interpreting this passage. One problem occurs in the second line, where the word 'purusha' can be interpreted either as 'a person' or as 'the indwelling principle of personality'. The other problem occurs in the fifth line, where the word 'this' is used to translate the Sanskrit 'etat'. The difficulty here is that 'etat' is neuter; and hence it cannot refer to any of the preceding nouns, which are all either masculine or feminine. So it is disconcertingly wide open to interpretation.

The following translation and retelling try to be more easily intelligible, by making specific choices that bring out one particular aspect of meaning. The word 'purusha' is translated as 'consciousness' (by identifying consciousness as the indwelling spirit of personality). And the word 'etat' ('this') is interpreted as referring specifically to 'living movement': or in other words to movement as animated by life. In Sanskrit (as described just above, in the previous section of this chapter), such a concept of animated movement is typically represented by the neuter noun 'jagat', to which 'etat' could thus be taken to refer.

Translation (from the Prashna Upanishad)	**Retelling** (from *FTU*, page 171)

<u>3.3</u>

This life is born from self. Just like some shadow-image [drawn] on consciousness, this [living movement] is drawn out upon the [self].	Each person's life is born from self, appearing like a moving image drawn by mind on consciousness.
By mind's activity, it comes to be in body here.	Through this activity of mind, life is expressed in body's acts.

Learning

As consciousness is expressed in the course of experience, a process of learning takes place, through a cyclic reflection of attention back and forth between consciousness and the perceived world.

- As attention *goes out* from consciousness towards the world, what has been learned from past experience is expressed – through understanding, feeling, thought and action – towards objects and events.

- When attention has thus turned to particular objects and events, consciousness continues to be expressed through perception, interpretation, judgement and comprehension: which assimilate new learning, through a *reflection* of attention *back* to underlying consciousness.

In the course of future experience, such assimilated learning is expressed in new understanding, feeling, thoughts and actions; and so the cycle continues, as illustrated in the following diagram:

OBJECTS AND EVENTS

	EXPRESSION		REFLECTION	
ACTION				PERCEPTION
THOUGHT		↑	↓	INTERPRETATION
FEELING				JUDGEMENT
UNDERSTANDING				COMPREHENSION

———————————————————————————————

C O N S C I O U S N E S S

This cycle of learning includes the entire process of life, in which all living faculties take part. Accordingly, life as a whole may be conceived as an ongoing process of learning and development, in which living experience is repeatedly 'breathed' out and in. From underlying consciousness, learning from past experience is 'breathed' out into the perceived world; thus giving rise to new experiences that are 'breathed' back in.

The traditional metaphor of 'vital breath', or 'prāṇa', was further used to describe a division of life into different vital faculties. In the Indian tradition in particular, the word 'prāṇa' is used in two ways. On the one hand, it is used to describe life as a continuing whole; and here it has the generic sense of 'ongoing life' or 'ongoing breath'. On the other hand, it was also used to describe five 'prāṇas' or 'vital faculties', each of which plays a particular part in the whole process of ongoing life.

One of these vital faculties was called 'apāna', which can be translated literally as the 'reverse breath'. A second was confusingly called 'prāṇa', where the term is not now being used in its generic sense of 'ongoing life' or 'ongoing breath', but in a more limited sense that can be translated literally as the 'forward breath'. The three remaining vital faculties were 'vyāna' (literally the 'discerning or disseminating breath'), 'udāna' (literally the 'ascending breath') and 'samāna' (literally the 'integrating breath').

These five vital faculties (the 'panca-prāṇas') have been explained rather differently in different texts and commentaries. In the following diagram, an attempt is made to interpret them as parts of the cycle of learning that has just been described above:

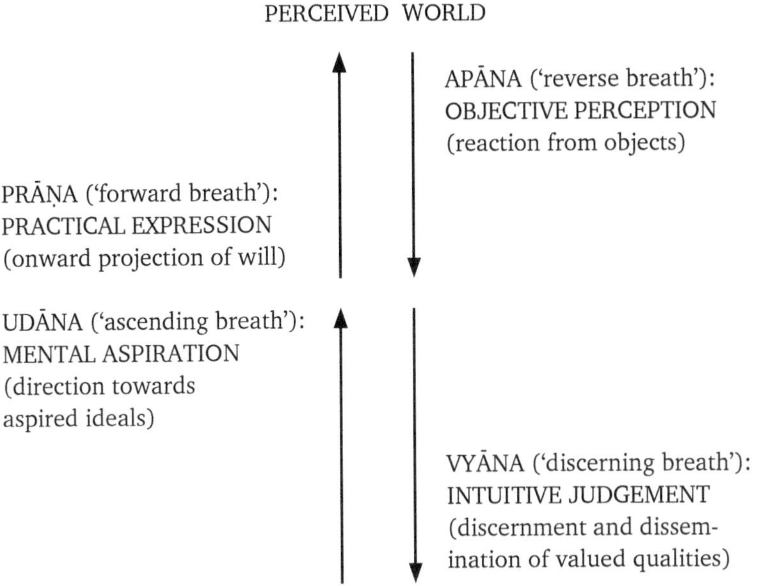

CONSCIOUSNESS

Essentially, the same interpretation of the five 'prāṇas' or 'vital breaths' is made in the following translation and retelling of the Prashna Upanishad, 3.4-12. As shown below in the translation of 3.5-6, the original text associates the vital breaths with various bodily organs in which they are supposed to act. However, such bodily organs, like the eyes or the mouth, are clearly meant to represent more subtle living faculties, like sight and speech, with which the vital breaths are more essentially associated. And further, as shown in 3.7 and 3.9-12, the text describes the vital breaths as essentially concerned with the process of ongoing experience: in which old experiences subside and lead on to new experiences, until a clarified understanding of life itself leads finally to undying truth.

The retelling modifies the original text by trying to interpret its bodily metaphors in terms of a more explicitly described cycle of living faculties, which express consciousness in the course of ongoing experience.

Translation (from the Prashna Upanishad)	**Retelling** (from *FTU*, pages 171-173)

3.4

As an emperor commands
his officers, telling each
to govern these villages
or those villages;

so too, this prāṇa [life]
appoints the other prāṇas
each to its own place.

As life expresses consciousness,
it carries out its purposes
through various different faculties
that are divisions of itself.

3.5-7

Apāna [is appointed]
to the excretory and
reproductive organs.

One of these faculties [apāna] reacts
to objects that have been perceived:
discarding waste, restricting aims,
and thus creating partial views
of world, as it appears perceived.

In eye and ear, together
with the mouth and nose,
prāṇa itself is established.

A second of these faculties [prāṇa]
looks on from what is now perceived:
projecting choices, from the past,
through life that carries on in time.

Samāna, however,
is in the middle;
for it leads
offered food
to assimilation.

A third among these faculties [samāna]
assimilates perceptions and
interpretations into knowledge
at the background of the mind:
where what is known is understood.
There, silent understanding knows,
unmoved by passing wants and needs
noised out by wish and fantasy.

From that arise
these seven flames
[perceptive faculties
lodged in the seven
orifices of the head
– two eyes, two ears,
two nostrils
and the mouth].

For, in the heart
is this self.

Here, there is this:
a hundred and
one channels;
from them a hundred
[offshoots] each;

in each of these [again]
seventy-two thousand
offshoot channels arise.

In these, moves vyāna.

Next, rising up
through one of these,
udāna leads:

through good
to a good world,
through ill to ill,
through both indeed
to the world of men.

A fourth among the faculties [vyāna]
goes circulating back and forth,
contrasting and comparing things:
thus judging valued qualities
and spreading subtle influence.

A fifth among the faculties [udāna]
expresses understanding which
has come from past experience: so
that learning may continue on.

3.8-9

Essentially,
the sun rises as prāṇa
[seen in the world]
outside;

for it is that which assists
the [inner] prāṇa
associated with the eye.

That which is this
divinity in earth
ties down
a person's apāna.

And [as for] that
which is in between:

pervading space,
that is samāna;

These different faculties relate
to different aspects of the world
that everyone experiences.

External choice that's mere reaction
corresponds to narrow objects
which attention has selected
from a world of many things.

Intention looking on through time
relates to processes of change,
by which all objects have been formed
and all objectives are achieved.

Understanding corresponds
to underlying principles,
continuing through change and difference
in the world's appearances.

the air is vyāna.

Discerning judgement corresponds
to qualities and values that
our feelings judge and thoughts compare
in the world that mind conceives.

Essentially, fire is udāna.
Thus, those in whom
[life's] fire has subsided
[go on to]
renewed becoming,

Expression rising from within
is manifest in outer world
by living energy of change:
which burns what's happened in the past,
thus forming new experiences.

with senses
taken into mind.

3.10

With what is thought,
one comes to life [prāṇa].

Life, joined to fire
and self, leads on
to world that thus
becomes conceived.

Each moment of our changing lives,
we come to life conditioned by
those influences from the past
that lead on to our future lives.

Whatever's learnt is thus reborn
from death of past experiences,
as seeming life keeps cycling on
from death to birth and birth to death.

3.11-12

Who knows life thus
is [truly] wise.
What comes from him
is never driven,
nor inadequate.

But underlying seeming life
conditioned by appearances,
what is the unconditioned ground
where life arises and returns
and living truly is alive?

He realizes
deathlessness.

As to that
there is this verse:

By questioning relentlessly
towards this unconditioned ground,
the self that knows all life is known
and deathless truth is realized.

'The origin of life,
its coming [here],
its standing place,

'and also its
fivefold extension,
and indeed its
self-related-ness:

'knowing [these],
one obtains
deathlessness.'

The living principle

What is the essential principle of life, shared in common by all living faculties and all the living acts of a person's body, senses and mind?

In the Kaushītaki Upanishad, 3.2-3, this essential living principle is identified as 'prajnyātman': which means 'the self that consists of consciousness' or, more briefly, 'the self of consciousness'.

Translation (from the Kaushītaki Upanishad)

Retelling (from *FTU*, pages 148-151)

From 3.2

... Some say:

'The living faculties
proceed towards
becoming one;

Each living personality
seems made of different faculties:
each one expressing consciousness
in its own ways, at its own times.

'for none alone
would be able
acting jointly
to make known:

And yet these different faculties
somehow express a unity
of knowledge that co-ordinates

'a name through speech,
a sight through seeing,
a sound through hearing,
a thought through mind.

names that are known by speaking them,
sights that are known by seeing them,
sounds that are known by hearing them,
thoughts that are known by thinking them.

'Essentially
becoming one,

As different objects are thus known
in different ways, at different times,
through different seeming faculties,

'the living faculties
arise, one by one,

'and make all
these things known.'

When speech speaks,
all faculties
are speaking there
along with it.

When sight sees,
all faculties
are seeing there
along with it.

When hearing hears,
all faculties
are hearing there
along with it.

When mind thinks,
all faculties
are thinking there
along with it.

That's how it is....
and yet, essentially,
belonging to
[all] living faculties,
there is
a higher principle.

these different ways of knowing things
reflect a unifying base
of underlying consciousness
on which each faculty depends.

Thus when speech speaks, all other
faculties are somehow understood
to be expressed in what is said.

Or when sight sees, all other
faculties are somehow understood
to be expressed in what is seen.

When hearing hears, all other
faculties are somehow understood
to be expressed in what is heard.

And when mind thinks, all other
faculties are somehow understood
to be expressed in what is thought.

Within these living faculties,
one common principle of life
is shared beneath their differences.

And this one living principle,
though from within, contains them all.

From 3.3

One lives
bereft of speech,
for we see the dumb.

What is essential to all life?

It cannot be the faculty
of speech; for there are those whom we
call 'dumb', who do not speak, but who
are still essentially alive.

One lives
bereft of sight,
for we see the blind.

One lives
bereft of hearing,
for we see the deaf.

One lives
bereft of mind,
for we see the infantile.

One lives
with arms cut off;

one lives
with legs cut off.

We say this
because, we say,
this is how we see it.

But then, in truth,
life in itself
is consciousness,
the [real] self,

which holds this
body all around
and causes it
to rise [alive].

Therefore, it is said,
one should heed
this alone
as the source (uktha).

This is the all-obtaining
in the breath of life.

Nor can it be the faculties
of sight or hearing; for we know
of those whom we call 'blind' or 'deaf',
who do not see or do not hear,
but who are still essentially alive.

And further too, we know of those
whose loss of outward sight or hearing
even strengthens inner life.

Nor can life's essence be the mind.
For can we say that life has gone,
where understanding is attained
and all mind's complex, changing acts
come to an end in simple truth?

Or can we say that life is missing,
where desires are achieved
and mind dissolves in happiness?

And can we say that life is absent
in the state of dreamless sleep,
where mind's perceptions, thoughts and feelings
all dissolve in rest and peace?

Life is essentially the source
from which all living acts arise.
It is the ground on which they stand,
and into which they are absorbed
when they return to source again.

Thus truly known, life in itself
is consciousness, the real self:
which holds this body all around
and causes it to rise, alive.

Essentially,
that which is
the breath of life
is consciousness.

And that which is
consciousness
is the breath of life....

Wherever life is seen in body,
consciousness is found implied.
Wherever consciousness is seen
expressed in body, so is life.

Thus 'life' and 'consciousness' are different
names for one same principle:
which makes this body seem alive,
and knows all that is ever known
in everyone's experience.

The impersonal basis of personality

'Human-ness'

In ordinary Sanskrit, as in many modern Indian languages, the word 'purusha' means 'a man' or 'a human being' or 'a person'. However, the word has also a special philosophical usage, which occurs over and over again in the Upanishads.

Thus philosophically used, the word 'purusha' does not refer to any particular man or human being or person, considered as a differentiated object among other objects in the world. Instead, in its philosophical usage, the word 'purusha' describes an essential principle of 'human-ness' which is shared in common by all different-seeming men, all different-seeming human beings and all different-seeming personalities.

As it is put in the Brihadāraṇyaka Upanishad, 2.5.18:

... sa vā	That, in truth,
ayam purushah	is this 'human-ness'
sarvāsu pūrshu	in all bodies:
purishayah ...	abiding [here] at rest within the body.

In this passage, the word used for 'body' is 'pur', which literally means 'a rampart wall' or 'a fortified enclosure' or 'a fortress' or 'a walled town or city'. The body is thus conceived as mere outward fortification: within which the inner principle called 'purusha' lives at peace, undisturbed by the conflicts and destructions of the outside world.

Moreover, this inner principle of 'human-ness' is not conceived to live only in some special bodies that we call 'human', to the exclusion of other bodies in the universe. Instead, all bodies and the entire universe are conceived to somehow express the same living principle which human beings find within themselves. Thus conceived, this same inner principle of 'human-ness' is to be found everywhere: expressed in all matter and all personality, throughout the universe.

Such a conception of all-embracing, all-pervading 'human-ness' is described in the following translation and retelling from the Brihadāraṇyaka Upanishad, 2.5 (of which the above quotation is a part).

<table>
<tr><td>Translation (from the
Brihadāraṇyaka Upanishad)</td><td>Retelling
(from FTU, pages 67-68)</td></tr>
</table>

<u>2.5.1</u>

This earth is the honey of all beings.	All creatures feed on fruit of earth; and earth, in turn, is fed by them.
To this earth, all beings are honey.	
This which is in this earth is radiant, deathless 'human-ness'.	Both in earth and in each person, that which shines and never dies is our common 'human-ness'.
And this which is the spiritual [principle] associated with the body is radiant, deathless 'human-ness'.	
This is just that which is this self.	This is the self each person is.
This is deathless. This is complete reality. This is all.	It is that same reality which always lives, unchanged, complete, in every partial-seeming thing.

<u>2.5.15</u>

That, in truth, is this self: the Lord of all beings, the King of all beings.	This self is lord and king of all.
Just as all the spokes of a chariot[-wheel] are fixed together at the hub and rim;	As in a wheel, all spokes are joined together at the hub and rim; so too, all things, all gods, all worlds, all lives, all separate-seeming selves are joined together in the self.

so too all beings,
all gods, all worlds,
all living energies
and all these selves
are fixed together
in the self.

From 2.5.18

... That, in truth,
is this 'human-ness'
in all our bodies:
abiding [here] at rest
within the body.

This, which lives in all our bodies,
is our common 'human-ness'.

There is nothing
uncontained by it;
nothing that is
not pervaded by it.

Outside this, there's no existence.
Nothing is, apart from this.

From 2.5.19

... 'It has become
the likeness of
form after form.

It is this that takes the likeness
of each form that is perceived.

'That is its form, for
observation round about.

'Through the powers
of illusion, Indra
[chieftain of the gods]
is arisen, many-formed;

From appearance thus created
come the many forms of God,
harnessing those many
different faculties of sense and action
which create our seeming world.

'for yoked of him
are [many] horses:
ten [of them],
hundreds [of them].'

This, in truth,
is the horses.

All our senses, all our bodies,
all the many, countless things
they see and touch, are nothing but
this one same self in each of us.

This, in truth, is the ten;
is the thousands;
many and unlimited.

That is this
complete reality:

with nothing that
can come before
or after it;

with no outside
and no inside.

It is that all-containing truth
with nothing else beside itself,
with nothing else before itself,
with nothing else that follows on,
with no outside and no inside.

This self is all reality,
experiencing everything.

Thus is the teaching.

Thus it is taught: *'This self is in
itself complete. It knows all things,
and all it knows is but itself.'*

Universal and individual

The philosophical concept of 'purusha', as 'human-ness', can be approached
in two, complementary ways.

• On the one hand, it may be approached universally: as a universal living
  principle that is found expressed in all personalities, in all minds and in
  all bodies, and thus in the universe as a whole.

• On the other hand, it may be approached individually: as the individual
  living principle that is found expressed in each particular personality, in
  each particular mind and in each particular body in the universe.

These two approaches are described in the following translation and retelling from the Shvetāshvatara Upanishad, chapter 3. This chapter describes
the part-mystical, part-philosophical conception of 'virāṭ purusha'; where
God is conceived as a universal personality: whose body is the totality of all
particular bodies in the world, whose mind is the sum total of all particular
minds, and whose self is the complete reality that underlies all physical and
mental phenomena throughout the universe.

Over and over again (in 3.2,7,11,13,18,20 and 21), the complete reality
of the universal self is explicitly identified with the inner principle of self
within each particular individual.

In the following translation, the word 'purusha' is translated as 'the principle of personality'.

Translation (from the Shvetāshvatara Upanishad)	**Retelling** (from *FTU*, pages 245-250)

<u>From 3.1</u>

It is the one with the net, ruling with its sovereign powers,	God is conceived to hold the web of circumstance, thus ruling all the world, with powers over everything.
ruling all the world with its powers;	
this which alone is one: in arising and in happening....	This universal principle, conceived as 'God', is one alone: in all that is created and in all that happens in the world.

<u>From 3.2</u>

... Not as second do they stand....	It has no second, as it stands here facing everyone within.
It stands facing people within themselves....	

<u>From 3.7</u>

Beyond that is the absolute, the great beyond.	It is complete reality, unlimited and ultimate.
[Here] individually in every body, it is hidden in all beings,	Found present individually within each body, it is known implicitly in everything.
the one [reality] containing all the world....	And yet it is one single unity, containing all the world.

<u>From 3.8</u>

I know this great principle of personality: pictured as the sun, beyond obscurity....	This all-containing principle is consciousness, known pictured as the self-illuminating sun, beyond all dark obscurity.

3.9

It's that
beyond which
there is nothing else,

Beyond it, there is nothing else.

than which
there's nothing smaller,
nothing greater.

There's nothing smaller, nothing greater.
Size does not apply to it,
nor any kind of quality.

Like a tree,
it stands as one,
unmoving,
in the place of light.

The manifested universe
is like a tree which seems to grow
a multiplicity of swaying
branches, rustling leaves and flowering
blossoms seen by outward sight.

But like a tree, examined at
the trunk where it supports itself,
the many-seeming world turns out
to be a single unity,
unmoving in the changeless ground.

This changeless ground is consciousness,
where the entire seeming tree
of universal happening
dissolves in unconditioned light.

By that principle
of personality,
all this [entire universe]
is filled.

All things, in truth, are only light
pervading all experience
of the entire universe.

3.10

That which is
above this [world]
has no form, and is
unaffected by all ill.

Transcending all appearances
perceived by body, sense and mind,
this principle of consciousness
is unattached to any form
and unaffected by all ill.

They who know this
become deathless.
But others go
to pain and misery.

Whoever knows it does not die.
All others lead a dying life
that leads to pain and misery.

<u>From 3.11</u>

Its are all faces, heads, necks. Its home is deep within each being's heart.	All faces, heads and bodies are mere instruments of consciousness, found here in every person's heart.
It is the all-pervading, blessed Lord....	It is the inner principle of spirit that pervades the world; and thus, it's worshipped as 'the Lord'.

<u>3.12</u>

The great Lord is truly this principle of personality:	It is the base of changeless light on which is founded order, justice, goodness, harmony, and guidance towards purity and truth.
setting goodness and ordered harmony in motion;	
and ruling the attainment of true purity, as changeless light.	

<u>From 3.13</u>

Measured by thumb, this principle is inner self:	Seen in each individual's own experience, this principle of consciousness is inner self:
living always in the heart of those that have been born;	the living centre of each individual personality. It's always present, living here within each person's mind and heart;
conceived through heart, through thought, through mind....	and it is found by turning thought to question back towards its source: back from the world, through mind and heart, towards the source where thoughts arise.

3.14

This [one] principle
has a thousand heads,
a thousand eyes,
a thousand feet.

As feelings, thoughts, perceptions change,
pure consciousness continues on.
It is the underlying ground
that's common to each one of them,
beneath their many differences
of quality and name and form.

And it's the same for everyone,
the common ground that stays the same
beneath all change and difference.

Because it underlies all differences
of quality and name and form,
there's nothing to distinguish it
from one experience to the next
or from one person to the next.

It is the common ground on which
we understand each other's acts;
as we communicate across
our physical and mental
differences, of body and of mind.

All hearts and minds and bodies, and
all feelings, thoughts, perceptions, acts,
express this common consciousness.

Encompassing the earth
on every side,
it stands beyond,
ten fingers breadth
beyond.

All of them are its instruments,
expressing it and thereby acting
for its sake; while it remains
beyond them all, the common background
of the many-seeming world.

3.15

This principle alone
is all this [world]:

All that is known, throughout the world,
is only known in consciousness.

what has been and
what is to be.

Thus, all that's known must be contained
entirely in consciousness;
and nothing really is outside.

Pure consciousness is all there is.

It's all the world's reality:
including all that's come to be
and everything that's yet to be.

It is at once
the Lord of deathlessness
and what grows
by food consumed.

It is at once the changeless light
that guides us on to deathlessness,
and the reality of world
where everything that's born and grows
is fed by death of other things.

3.16

Its hands and feet
are everywhere;

eyes, head and face
are everywhere;

its ears
are everywhere.

Encompassing everything
in the [entire] world,
it stands.

Whatever's known expresses it,
no matter where or when perceived.

All happenings are its faculties:
expressing it and thereby acting
for its sake; while it remains
beyond them all, the changeless background
of all changing happenings.

3.17

Lighting all
qualities perceived
through any faculty,

it has itself
no faculties
that act in any way.

It's chief and Lord,
the great refuge
of all.

It lights all of the qualities
that every faculty perceives:

but it is not itself attached
to any faculty at all;
for in itself it does not act.

All faculties and all their acts
depend on it to be perceived,
to focus and co-ordinate;

but it does not depend on them.

It is their central principle:
their origin and common ground,
their guiding light and stable base
enabling ordered harmony,
their final goal and place of rest.

3.18

The swan[-like spirit],   The self that's found embodied here,
here embodied   within each person, is expressed
in the stronghold   outside as well, in nature's play
of nine gates,   of circumstance and happening.
is at play outside:

as the source   Remaining in itself unmoved,
of all desire,   it is the inner principle
                                  from which all motivation comes.

controlling the   All movements and all standing still,
entire world   no matter where or when perceived,
of fixed and   are understood expressing it;
moving things.   reflecting back to self within.

3.19

With neither feet   It has no feet, yet it keeps up
nor hands,   with all that moves. It has no hands,
yet moving fast and   yet it grasps all experience.
grasping [everything];

it sees without eyes,   It's that which sees and hears; without
hears without ears.   the faculties of seeing sights
                                  and hearing sounds, of objects in
                                  some alien world outside itself.

What's to be known,   It's that which knows whatever's known.
it knows;

but there is no knower   But it is not an object known
[other than itself]   by anyone who knows of it
that knows of it.   through faculties and instruments
                                  that act towards a world outside.

It is called
'the great, primeval
purusha [the principle
of personality]'.

Conceived as the 'I'-principle,
it's what each person really is:

pure, unconditioned consciousness,
known prior to all attributes
superimposed by partial sight.

3.20

Subtler than subtle,
greater than great,
is the self:

set down [here]
in the living creature's
cave [of heart].

Far subtler than all subtlety,
far greater than all magnitude
that senses see or mind conceives,
the self is found established here
in every living creature's heart.

Freed
from grief and misery
by the Ordainer's grace,
one sees that [self],

unmixed with purpose
and desire,

Set free from grief and misery
by gift of grace transcending
little ego's petty purposes,
one knows the self desireless:

as the Lord
in all his majesty.

as that which stands beyond all acts
of power and greatness in the world.

3.21

This unaging, ageless
self of all
is what I know,

[seen] going everywhere
through its
pervading sovereignty.

This same unaging, ageless self
is all that's ever truly known:

perceived extending everywhere
through its pervading sovereignty.

Those who discuss reality
speak of it as ending birth.

They speak of it
as timeless and continual.

It's spoken of as ending birth;
for where it's known all time dissolves
in deathless continuity.

Inner light

What is the essential principle of personality that is called 'purusha'?

In the Brihadāraṇyaka Upanishad, 5.6.1, it is identified as 'bhāh satyas tasminn antar-hridaye' or 'the true light within the heart'.

Translation (from the Brihadāraṇyaka Upanishad)	**Retelling** (from *FTU*, page 100)

5.6.1

This purusha, associated with the mind, is the true light within the heart,	The essence of this personality that seems to rise from mind is nothing else but light itself, found here within each person's heart;
like a grain of rice or barley.	just as the essence of a plant that seems to rise and grow from seed is nothing else but life itself, somehow contained within each seed.
It is the Lord of all, the ruler of all: governing all this, all this whatsoever.	This inner principle of light guides all experience, and hence governs everything that we perceive, beneath whatever seems to be.

Underlying consciousness

In the following translation and retelling from the Kaṭha Upanishad, 5.8-15, 'purusha' is further identified as underlying consciousness, continuing through the changes and variations of world and personality.

Translation (from the Kaṭha Upanishad)	**Retelling** (from *FTU*, pages 31-34)

5.8

This, which is awake in those that sleep, is purusha [the inner principle],	What is the individual life principle that carries on behind the changing mask of seeming personality? It is

just this: which always is awake,
while other things dissolve in sleep.

producing forth
desire on desire.

From it arises each desire
that seeks some narrow, passing goal,
and thus clouds personality
with incompleteness seeking change.

It alone
is clear and stainless.

But in itself it's always clear;
for it is all reality:
which stays the same, undimmed, unchanged,
beneath all mere appearances.

It alone
is all reality.

It alone
may be called 'deathless'.

It's that alone which does not die.

In it,
all worlds are based.

In it, all seeming worlds are based.
Apart from it, there's nothing else.

Nothing at all
transcends it.

This is just that.

5.9-10

Just as one fire,
permeating the universe,
has become the likeness
of form after form;

Just as one common principle
of underlying energy
is there throughout the universe,
appearing in the different forms
that are so differently perceived
in different objects and events;

so too, one self
within all beings
has the likeness
of form after form,
and is outside as well.

so too, one common principle
of underlying consciousness
is here throughout experience,
appearing in the different forms
that are so differently perceived
in different personalities.

Just as one air,
permeating the universe,
has become the likeness
of form after form;

This underlying consciousness,
which different people share alike
beneath all their conditionings,
is every person's real self.

so too, one self
within all beings
has the likeness
of form after form,
and is outside as well.

It's here in body, sense and mind
and yet it is beyond them all.

5.11

Just as the sun,
the whole world's sight,
is not affected
by outside,
defective sights;

Just as the sun lights what we see,
quite unaffected by the failings
of a person's sense of sight;

so too, the one
self in all beings
is not affected
by world's misery.

so too, the self lights all experience,
unaffected by the failings
of perception, thought and feeling
in our senses and our minds.

It is outside.

5.12

It is the one
controller,

the self within
all beings;

In course of time, as different actions,
thoughts and feelings come and go,
they are co-ordinated by
this underlying consciousness
of self, which is their common base
beneath their seeming differences.

This is the common basis where
all different persons, and the
various objects that they see, relate.

It is from here that different things
and different persons are seen
functioning together, in an
ordered and intelligible world.

which makes
the one seed
manifold.

And it is only this, one self
of underlying consciousness,
whose essence is made manifest
in all the many forms of world.

The steadfast see it
standing in itself.

To them,
as not to others,
lasting happiness
[is found].

*By turning inwards, this one truth
is seen, already standing here:
as one's own self. Just this, and
only this, brings lasting happiness.*

5.13

It is the continuity
of changing things;

the consciousness
of conscious things;

the one among the many;

that which fulfils desires.

It is the continuity
that is implied by changing things;

the changeless base of consciousness
implied by changing mental states;

the changeless, partless unity
which all diversity implies,
and which alone fulfils desire.

The steadfast see it
standing in itself.

To them,
as not to others,
lasting peace
[is found].

*By turning inwards, this one truth
is seen, already standing here:
as one's own self. Just this, and
nothing else but this, brings lasting peace.*

5.14

It is conceived as
'that is this';

It is conceived as 'that out there':
as all the world's reality
beneath all mere appearances.

And it's conceived as 'this in here':
as ever-present consciousness,
by which appearances are known.

But both of these, 'this' consciousness
and 'that' reality, are always
present here together: at all times,
in everyone's experience.

Thus being always here together,
they can never be distinguished.
Though we call them by two names,
they are not two, but only one.

the undefinable,
supreme happiness.

This final non-duality,
of knowing self and all that's known,
is unconditioned happiness;
for here completeness has been found.

How then
may I know that,

whether it
shines [directly]

or shines back
[reflected]?

How then can it be truly known,
as it shines out from self within
and is reflected back from world?

5.15

There the sun
does not shine,
nor moon and stars;

nor do these
lightning flashes shine;
much less this fire.

It does not shine by light of sun
or moon or stars or burning fire.
It shines alone, by its own light.

It alone shining,
everything
shines after it.

Without it, nothing else can shine;
for it lights all appearances:
which shine as its reflected light.

By its light,
everything here
shines back.

Thus all the world is nothing else
but the reflected light of self.

As self illuminates the world,
it just illuminates itself.

Through all the world's appearances,
this self-illuminating light
remains always unchanged, unmixed
with anything beside itself.

The unborn source

In various accounts of creation in the Vedas and the Upanishads, 'purusha' is described as the unborn source and the underlying basis of the apparent universe. These accounts contain a curious mixture of myth and philosophy, which can make them seem paradoxical and self-contradictory.

* On the one hand, 'purusha' is mythically described as having a personal form: with bodily features such as a head and eyes, and with mental features like thought and will.

* On the other hand, this same 'purusha' is philosophically described as unchanging and impersonal: without form or faculties or mind.

These contradictions may be seen in the following translation of the Muṇḍaka Upanishad, 2.1 (specifically in 2.1.2 and 2.1.4). In the retelling reproduced alongside the translation, an attempt is made to avoid some of the apparent contradiction, by a philosophical interpretation of the mythical metaphor. In particular, 'purusha' is interpreted as an impersonal principle of unchanging, invariant consciousness: which underlies the changes and variations of personality.

Translation (from the Muṇḍaka Upanishad)

Retelling (from *FTU*, pages 190-192)

2.1.1

'That is this truth.

'As from a blazing fire, thousands of sparks issue forth, similarly formed;	'As sparks come forth from blazing fire; so too our many seeming lives arise from one same consciousness, shine out as only consciousness, and as they seem to fade away leave nothing else but consciousness.
'so too, dear friend, from that which does not change,	
'manifold beings are born forth and go back there again.	

<u>2.1.2</u>

'For purusha is divine
[transcendent and
self-luminous],

'and has no bodied form.

'It is outside and inside,
the unborn [principle]
of radiant purity:

'unmixed with mind,
unmixed with breath
and vital faculties.

'It transcends
transcendent
changelessness.

'This principle of unmixed light
shines out unchanged from deep within
each changing form of bodied life,

gives life to every breath we take,
and lights the seeming world outside.

'It has itself no bodied form.
It has no birth. It has no breath.
It has no mind, nor faculties.

'It is beyond all we conceive
as here or there, or anywhere.

<u>2.1.3</u>

'From it is born:

'life-breath and mind
and all sense-faculties;

'the ether, air, light,
water, and the
all-supporting earth.

'From it is born all life, all mind,
all feeling, thought, perception, sense,
all principles, all qualities,
all meanings, all the changing forms
and all the many varied things
of which the universe seems made.

<u>2.1.4-5</u>

'Fire is its head;
its eyes
the moon and sun;
the directions are its ears.

'Its speech is
the revealed Vedas;
the air, its living breath.

'Its heart is all
the universe.
From its feet,
[it is] the earth.

'The world is known by consciousness;
the world is seen by consciousness;
all meanings are but consciousness;
all qualities are consciousness;

'and everything that feelings feel,
or thoughts conceive, or senses see,
is nothing else but consciousness.

'The world stands but in consciousness,
which is each person's real self.

'For, of all beings,
it is the self within.

'From it [comes] fire
whose fuel is the sun.

'From the moon [come]
rain, plants on earth.

'The male sheds seed
in the female.

'From purusha,
many offspring
are originated.

'The blazing sun is consciousness;
the moon's cool light is consciousness;
dark clouds and rain are consciousness;
the solid earth and all the crops
and food it bears are consciousness.

'And all the many, varied forms
of life we creatures seem to lead,
here born and fed upon the earth,
are only forms of consciousness.

2.1.6-8

'From it [come]
hymns and chants
and ritual verses,
consecrations, sacrifices,

'and all ceremonies,
sacrificial gifts,
the calendar,
the sacrificer,

'and the worlds
where the moon
or where the sun
illuminates and clarifies.

'And from it,
in many ways,

'the gods are
brought forth;

'the accomplished
celestials;

'humans, beasts and birds;

'the forward and
reverse life-breaths;

'From consciousness comes all we say,
all that we do, all we express,
all speech, all poetry, all song,

'all acts, intentions, purposes,
all we perceive or think or feel,
all energy, vitality,
all justice, truth and happiness.

'rice and barley;

'intent, faith, truth,
chastity and law.

'The seven vital breaths
come forth from it;
the seven flames, the fuel,
the seven offerings;

'these seven worlds
where move
the living energies
laid down [here]
in the cave [of the heart],
seven by seven.

2.1.9

'From it, all oceans
and all mountains;

'from it flow
rivers of all forms.

'And from it, all plants
and the essential flavour
by which it stands
[associated] with
the elements of world.

'For it is
the self within.

'Upon this base of consciousness,
great-seeming mountains are perceived,
and different rivers seem to flow
through different regions of the earth
to join the oceans' vast expanse.

'In consciousness all forms arise:
all object-forms, all forms of life,
all solid things, all changing flow,
all gross and subtle elements
of body and of mind in which
we seem to find our inner selves.

2.1.10

'Purusha alone is
the entire universe,
action, intent,
complete reality,
the deathless ultimate.

'This principle of consciousness,
this single principle alone
is all there is: all of the world
our outward senses seem to see,

'One who knows this,
that's seated in
the cave [of heart],

'cuts through the knot
of ignorance,
here [in this life],
dear friend....'

'all action in this outside world,
all purpose that may be expressed,
all meaning that our thoughts conceive,
all value that emotion feels.

'This deathless, final principle
of consciousness is here and now
within each heart: for each of us,
the centre of experience.

'Whoever realizes it
undoes all seeming ignorance....'

The unmoved mover

In the Kena Upanishad, chapter 1, though the word 'purusha' is not explicitly used, there is an interesting description which throws some light on the concept of 'purusha': as an unchanging, impersonal principle that is expressed in all movement and all personality.

As shown in the following translation and retelling, there is something of a correspondence here with the Aristotelian concept of the 'unmoved mover'. This concept is usually taken to be a way of describing 'God': as the underlying principle of the entire universe. But Aristotle also used this same concept to describe the 'soul': as the underlying principle of each individual personality. Such a complementarity of universal and individual interpretations applies to the Kena Upanishad as well.

Translation (from the
Kena Upanishad)

Retelling
(from *FTU*, pages 135-137)

<u>1.1</u>

By what motivated
does the mind
fly motivated forth?

What motivates mind's changing show
of seeming objects, thoughts, desires?

What makes the mind go out to things
that seem to be outside itself?

What sends the mind, in soaring flight,
to search for freedom, happiness?

From what does mind come down again,
to earth: where joy seems always bound
to pettiness and suffering?

By what enjoined   What joins together various acts –
does the primal   of body, sense and mind – to make
breath of life   each person's individual life?
go forth?

By what motivated   From what does meaning come: into
do they speak   the things we do, the words we speak,
this speech?   the gestures that our bodies make?

Sight, hearing: What common light co-ordinates
what intelligence   our differing perceptions
enjoins them?   into fuller knowledge of the world?

1.2

It's that which is: One common, inner principle
                           of consciousness is found in life,
the hearing [principle]   in mind and senses, words and acts.
of hearing,

the thinking [principle]
of thought,

the very speaking
[principle] of speech,

the essential living
[principle] of life,

the seeing [principle]
of sight.

Becoming free,   Those who are brave break free from world's
the steadfast   appearances, and realize
leave the world behind   that self is unmixed consciousness:
and come to deathlessness. beyond all seeming change and death.

1.3

There, seeing does not go;   This truth cannot be reached by mind
nor does speech,   or senses, nor described by speech.
nor mind.

We do not know,
we don't discern,
how it could be taught.

Nor can such faculties explain
the way in which it may be taught.

1.4

It is quite other
than the known;

and further, it's
beyond the unknown.

In truth, the self, as consciousness,
is not an object that is known;
nor is it anything unknown.

This we have heard
from the ancients,
who have thus
explained it for us.

Its knowledge comes from ancient times.
Its knowledge comes before all time;
for it must first be known before
the very thought of time can rise.

From 1.5

It is not that
which rises up
from words and speech.

It isn't something conjured up
by words and thoughts; instead, it is
the ever-present, knowing ground:

It's that from which
words and speech arise....

from which all thoughts and words arise,
on which all thoughts and words depend,
to which all thoughts and words return.

From 1.6

It's that which is
not thought by mind;

[but] that by which
the mind is thought,
they say....

It isn't something thought by mind;
instead, it is the principle
of consciousness that lights the mind:
by which all mind and thoughts are known.

From 1.7-8

It's that which is
not seen by sight;
[but] that by which
sight is seen....

It isn't something seen by sight,
or heard by listening; instead,
it is the knowing principle
that lights all sight and sound and sense.

It's that which is
not heard by hearing;
[but] that by which
hearing is heard....

<u>1.9</u>

It's that which is   It isn't something breathed by breath
not breathed by breath   or lived by life; instead, it is
or lived by life;   the living principle by which
                                  all breath and life are vitalized.
[but] that by which
breath is breathed
and life is lived.

Just that   This knowing principle of life
is the reality   is not a partial object, not
which you must know;   some little part of world, to which
                                  our minds and senses can attend.
not this
[world of objects]   Instead, it is the common ground
to which this   of all appearances that show
[personality]   some part of world, perceived
pays heed.   by partial body, sense and mind.

                                  This common ground is all there is.
                                  It is complete reality,
                                  which each appearance shows in part.

                                  It's known in full as knowing self:
                                  as pure, unchanging consciousness
                                  beneath all personality.

One's own self

In the following translation and retelling from the Kaṭha Upanishad, 6.17, the individual approach is described: as a focussing of attention inward, towards the essential core of pure, unconditioned self within each personality. This inner principle is to be found most directly by turning attention back into one's own experience: thus seeking out the true essence of one's own self, unobscured by the outward mask of ego's changing attributes.

Translation (from the Kaṭha Upanishad)	**Retelling** (from *FTU*, page 41)

<u>6.17</u>

Measured by thumb, purusha [the principle of personality] is inmost self:	The real self, the inmost principle of personality, is always present here at heart in everyone's experience.
living always in the heart of those that have been born.	
With steadfast courage, one should choose that out, from one's own personality;	Each petty ego lives in fear for its own false security that clings to passing attributes of changing personality.
[just as the inner] arrow-shaft [is drawn out] from [a reed of] munja grass.	But, putting ego's fears aside with steadfast courage, one may choose from one's own personality that inner, unconditioned core which does not fear or change or die and is one's true security.
That one should know, as deathless purity.	
That one should know, as deathless purity.	

The 'I'-principle

How can one find the essential, impersonal principle of self within one's own personality?

In the Prashna Upanishad, 4.9-10, a progressive enquiry is suggested: from outward faculties of sense, through inward faculties of thought and discernment, towards the inmost ground of unconditioned, changeless consciousness that underlies all our conditioned and changing faculties.

It is this unconditioned ground that the word 'purusha' finally indicates, as the true principle which each person calls 'I'.

Translation (from the Prashna Upanishad)

Retelling (from *FTU*, pages 177-178)

4.9

For this is the see-er,
the toucher, the hearer,
the smeller, the taster,

It is the inner principle
of all our different faculties.

It lights all seeing from within.
It's that which is aware in touch.
From it, all meaning is expressed;
it shows all meaning heard in sound.
And it discerns all taste and smell.

the minder,
the thinker,
the creator,
the knowing self,

It is the thinking principle,
the knowing subject of the mind:
which carries on through passing states,
as thoughts and feelings come and go.

purusha [the principle
of personality].

It is the common principle
within a person's changing acts.

It is established
in the ultimate,
unchanging self.

And thus, for everyone, it is
the changeless self that carries on
through all the different acts it knows.

It's for this self that acts are done.

This principle of knowing self
is what each person really is.

It's that which everyone calls 'I'.

From 4.10

One who truly
comes to know
that which is imageless,
bodiless, uncoloured,
changeless clarity;

It has no image in itself.
Nor has it any kind of body,
nor conditioned qualities.

[such a one] attains
to this same
changeless ultimate.

[Such a] one,
dear friend,
then knowing all,
becomes all....

As pure, unchanging consciousness,
it is the unconditioned ground
of all conditioned faculties
and all the world that they perceive.

Whoever comes to know this self
finds all the world's reality
and realizes everything.

Self

Turning back in

Quite plainly and simply, the Sanskrit word 'ātman' is equivalent to the English word 'self'. This is so both in classical Sanskrit and in the modern Indian languages that derive from Sanskrit. And further, it is so not only in the ordinary, unquestioning usage of everyday life, but also in the reflective usage of philosophical enquiry, where reason turns back to question the very assumptions from which it proceeds.

One such habitual assumption is that a person's self consists of a body, a set of senses and a mind, which are part of a larger world outside. But then, if self is just an object in the world, how can the world be known by it? Or, if self is not just an object, then what else can it be? And how can it be known?

The word 'ātman' is derived from the root 'an', meaning 'to breathe' or 'to live'. In the Rig Veda, it has an early form 'tman', meaning 'the vital breath'. In accordance with this derivation and early usage, the word 'ātman' describes the self as an inner, spiritual principle of life: quite distinct from the outward personality that is seen to act in the external world.

In the Kaṭha Upanishad, 4.1, the true nature of the self is described as 'pratyag-ātman': which means literally 'the turned-back self' or, to elaborate a little, 'the self, returned to self [to its own true reality]'.

Translation (from the Kaṭha Upanishad)	**Retelling** (from *FTU*, page 26)
<u>4.1</u>	
The self-becoming excavated outward-going apertures [of sense].	It seems our senses are created looking out: from self within towards a world that's known outside.
Thus one sees outwards, not towards the self within.	And so, it seems we only see external objects in the world, as they appear to outward sense.

At first, it seems there is no way
to see the self that knows within,
the self from which all seeing comes.

But one brave person, | But one brave person, seeking
seeking deathlessness, | deathlessness, turned sight back in, towards
turned sight back in | the inner source from which sight comes;
upon itself;

and thus the self was truly seen:
and saw the self, | as unconditioned consciousness,
returned to self | from which all seeming things arise.
[to its own
true reality].

Unbodied light

What is there to be found by turning back within?

In the following story from the Chāndogya Upanishad, 8.7-12, a progressive enquiry is described, through the three states of waking, dream and sleep. At each stage, persistent questioning shows up the inadequacy of previous understanding; until the nature of the self is shown at last to be pure consciousness: unconditioned by the gross external body that appears in the waking state, or by the subtle body of imagination and feeling that appears in dream, or even by the absence of body that appears in the seeming nothingness of deep sleep.

Translation (from the **Retelling**
Chāndogya Upanishad) (from *FTU*, pages 126-134)

<u>8.7.1</u>

'That which is self | 'The real self, in each of us,
dispels [all] ill; | is stainless, undecaying,
 | free from hunger, free from thirst,
'is untouched | untroubled in the midst of grief.
by age, decay
and death and grief;

'does not hunger,
does not thirst.

'It's that for which
all thought and all desire
is only truth.

'It's that which is
to be sought out;
that which we
must seek to know.

'Whoever finds
and knows that self
attains all worlds
and all desires.'

Thus said Prajāpati
[Lord of created things].

'It has no thought nor wish, but truth.
This is the self we cannot help but seek,
the truth we seek to understand.

'Whoever sees and knows this self
gains all the world, and finds
the goal of all desires.'

These words, the gods and demons heard,
were said by Lord Prajāpati,
the Lord of all created things.

8.7.2

That, both the gods
and demons heard.

They said: 'Well,
let us seek that self:
that self which seeking
one attains all worlds
and all desires.'

Of the gods, Indra
himself went forth;
of the demons, Virocana.

The two came
independently,
with sacrificial fuel
in their hands, into
the presence of Prajāpati.

To seek this self that gains the world
and finds the goal of all desire,
the gods and demons sent their chiefs
to question him that made the world.

Thus Indra, chief among the gods,
and demon-king Virocana
left home and came, in search of truth,
before their Lord Prajāpati.

Each came with fuel grasped in hand,
to show their wish that ignorance
should burn in sacrificial flame.

<u>8.7.3</u>

Thirty-two years
they lived the chaste
and humble life
of student discipline.

Prajāpati said to them:
'Seeking what, have you
been living [here]?'

'"That which is self
dispels [all] ill;

'"is untouched
by age, decay
and death and grief;

'"does not hunger,
does not thirst.

'"It's that for which
all thought and all desire
is only truth.

'"It's that which is
to be sought out;
that which we
must seek to know.

'"Whoever finds
and knows that self
attains all worlds
and all desires."

'Sir, these words are
made known as yours.

'We live [here]
seeking that.'

They put aside their finery,
their shining ornaments and crowns,
their life of outward wealth and power.

Thirty-two years they lived instead
the humble life of supplicants,
who would prepare themselves to learn.

Until at last Prajāpati
asked: 'What is it you wish to know?'

They said: 'We've heard that you describe
a stainless, undecaying self
by which desires are attained.
This self is what we wish to find.'

<u>8.7.4 and 8.8.1</u>

Prajāpati spoke to them.

'This that is seen in sight
is purusha [the knowing
principle of personality].

'This is the self', he said.
'It does not die;
nor has it fear.
It is the absolute.'

'Then, Sir, what is it
that's perceived
in water,
or in a mirror?'

'Just this itself
is perceived within
all these', he said.

'Look at [your] self
in a pan of water
and then tell me
what it is of self
that you don't know.'

They looked into
a pan of water.

Then, Prajāpati
said to them:
'What do you see?'

They said: 'Sir, we see
it all: the self
that's pictured [here],
down to the hairs
and fingernails.'

'Then what you seek is close at hand,'
was the reply. 'For self is seen
where sight looks back into itself.
It is the changeless absolute,
where death and fear do not arise.'

'But Sir,' they asked, 'what is it that
a person sees reflected in
the stillness of a shining pool
or in a mirror's clarity?'

'See for yourselves,' was the reply.
'One same reality is seen
in everything. Go look into
a pool of water, and then say
what you may find reflected there.'

Thus, Indra and Virocana
went to a nearby pool and looked
and said: 'We see of course ourselves,
down to our hair and fingernails.'

<u>8.8.2-3</u>

Next, Prajāpati said
to them: 'Becoming
well-adorned,
well-dressed,
well-groomed,

'[then] look into
the pan of water.'

Becoming well-adorned,
well-dressed,
well-groomed,
they made to look
into the pan of water.

Prajāpati now
asked them:
'What do you see?'

They said: 'Sir, just as
we are well-adorned,
well-dressed,
well-groomed;

'so too, these [reflections],
Sir, are well-adorned,
well-dressed,
well-groomed.'

'This is the self,' he said.
'It does not die,
nor has it fear.
It is the absolute.'

They went away,
content at heart.

Prajāpati then said to them:

'Now dress in all your finery,
put on your crowns and ornaments;
then look again into the pool
and say what is reflected there.'

They dressed and looked and said with pride:
'We see ourselves as we should be,
dressed as befits our kingly state.'

Prajāpati's reply was brief:

'Whatever you may think you see,
all that you see is only self.
It is complete reality,
where death and fear do not arise.'

Then satisfaction seemed to dawn
on Indra and Virocana.
It seemed that there was nothing left
to learn; and so they took their leave
and made their way towards their homes.

<u>8.8.4</u>

Looking after them,
Prajāpati said:

But, as they left, Prajāpati
looked sadly after them and thought:

'They go away
not having reached
or understood the self.

'They haven't understood at all.
Their faith clings on to false beliefs.
Whoever lives by such belief
stays caught in futile misery.'

'Whoever holds
this doctrine, be they
gods or demons,
shall be overcome.'

Quite satisfied at heart,
Virocana went
to the demons; and
to them proclaimed
this doctrine:

Virocana, triumphantly,
went back into his demon world,
where he proclaimed: 'Our selves come first!

'Let us be strong, increase our power,
and take by force what we desire.
Let's feed and clothe and arm ourselves,
to satisfy our needs and build
our strength to do just as we please.

'Here self alone
is to be magnified;
[and] self is to be served.

'Here magnifying
self alone
and serving self,

'For it befits our demon state
that world be bent to serve our needs
and wishes, as embodied selves.'

'one attains both worlds:
this world and
that beyond.'

<u>8.9.1</u>

But Indra, before he had
quite reached the gods,
saw this anxiety:

But Indra, on his way back home,
was troubled by a nagging doubt:

'Just as this [bodily self]
becomes well-adorned
in the well-adorned body,

'If self is body, it enjoys
good fortune as the body does.

'[becomes] well-dressed
in the well-dressed [body],

'When body is well-dressed ... so too
is self; when body gains in wealth
and power and grace ... so too does self.

'[becomes] well-groomed
in the well-groomed
[body];

'so too, it becomes

'blind in the [body
that is] blind,

'lame in the [body
that is] lame,

'crippled in the [body
that is] crippled.

'And, consequent upon
the destruction
of the body,
it is destroyed.

'I see no satisfaction here.'

'But, when the body's eyes are dimmed,
when body's wealth and power fade,
when grace departs; then it would seem …

'that self, like body, must decay,
that self, like body, suffers loss
of sight and wealth and power and grace.

'I *can't* be satisfied with this.'

<u>8.9.2-3</u>

Fuel in hand,
he came back again.

Thus Indra turned and went again
before his Lord Prajāpati,
again with fuel grasped in hand
to show his unburned ignorance.

Prajāpati said to him:

'Maghavan, since you
went off, content at heart,
together with Virocana,
seeking what
have you returned?'

'What brings you back? You seemed so pleased
when, just a little while ago,
you left with King Virocana.'

[Indra] said:
'Just as this [bodily self]
becomes well-adorned
in the well-adorned body,

'[becomes] well-dressed
in the well-dressed [body],

Indra explained his troubled doubt,
and lived for thirty-two more years
a student's dedicated life;

'[becomes] well-groomed
in the well-groomed
[body];

'so too, it becomes

'blind in the [body
that is] blind,

'lame in the [body
that is] lame,

'crippled in the [body
that is] crippled.

'And, consequent upon
the destruction
of the body,
it is destroyed.

'I see no satisfaction here.'

'It is just so, Maghavan,'
said [Prajāpati].
'However, I will explain
it further to you.

'Live [here] another
thirty-two years.'

[Indra] then lived [there]
another thirty-two years.

To him, [Prajāpati] spoke.   until Prajāpati spoke out
again, in different words, about
the truth that Indra wished to learn:

8.10.1-4

'This which journeys   'Where body's world
free in dream,   dissolves in dream
enabling mind to magnify;   and mind is free,
    the self shines there.

    'It is the deathless,
    fearless absolute.'

'this is the self', he said.
'It does not die;
nor has it fear.
It is the absolute.'

Then [Indra] went away,
content at heart.
But, before he had
quite reached the gods,
he saw this anxiety:

'It's true that even if
this body becomes blind,
the [dream self] does
not become blind;

'if [the body
becomes] lame,
the [dream self] does
not become lame.

'Indeed, it doesn't
suffer from the ills
of this [body].

'Not by the slaying
of this [body] is
the [dream self] slain.

'Not by the lameness
of this [body]
is it lame.

'And yet [in dream],
it is as if they kill it,
as if they strip it,

'as if it comes to know
unpleasantness,
as if it weeps as well.

'I see no satisfaction here.'

Fuel in hand,
he came back again.

And now to Indra, once again,
it seemed that he had understood.

He took his leave and started out
towards his home. But on his way
a further doubt disturbed his mind
and brought him back to learn some more;

again with fuel in his hand,
by which he showed his wish to burn
the ignorance that still remained.

Prajāpati said to him:
'Maghavan, since you
went off, content at heart,
seeking what
have you returned?'

Prajāpati asked: 'What is it
that brings you back again so soon?'

Indra said:
'It's true that even if
this body becomes blind,
the [dream self] does
not become blind;

Indra explained: 'The self in dream
may not be bound to suffer those
same ills that trouble body in
the waking world of outer things.

'if [the body
becomes] lame,
the [dream self] does
not become lame.

'When outward eyes no longer see
and body has thus lost its sight,
the self in dreams still seems to see.
And when gross, outward body dies,
perhaps the self lives on in dream.

'Indeed, it doesn't
suffer from the ills
of this [body].

'Not by the slaying
of this [body] is
the [dream self] slain.

'Not by the lameness
of this [body] is it lame.

'And yet [in dream],
it is as if they kill it,
as if they strip it,

'But, even in the state of dreams,
the self does not seem fully free.
In many dreams, self seems to fear,
seems to be driven, hunted down;
it seems in pain, it seems to weep,
it seems to suffer death and grief.

'as if it comes to know
unpleasantness,
as if it weeps as well.

'I see no satisfaction here.'

'I *can't* be satisfied with this.'

'It is just so, Maghavan,'
said [Prajāpati].
'However, I will explain
it further to you.

So Indra stayed for thirty-two
more years again; and when this time
had passed away, Prajāpati
spoke out these words that he might learn:

'Live [here] another
thirty-two years.'

[Indra] then lived [there]
another thirty-two years.

To him, [Prajāpati] spoke.

8.11.1-2

'That is this,
where one who sleeps
perceives no dream,

'[but is] withdrawn
back in to unity
and peace.

'In depth of sleep
which knows no dream,
self shines as peace.

'It is the fearless,
deathless absolute.'

'This is the self,' he said.
'It does not die;
nor has it fear.
It is the absolute.'

Then [Indra] went away,
content at heart.
But, before he had
quite reached the gods,
he saw this anxiety:

Yet once again, it seemed that truth
had dawned in Indra's searching mind.
But yet again, returning home,
poor Indra's mind was seized by doubt.

'This [deep sleep self],
such as it is,

'does not rightly
know itself,
face to face,
as "I am this";

'nor [does it know]
these things
created in the world.

'It [thus] becomes
a something
that has gone
into complete
annihilation.

'I see no satisfaction here.'

Fuel in hand,
he came back again.

Prajāpati said to him:

'Maghavan, since you
went off, content at heart,
seeking what
have you returned?'

And yet again, his wish to burn
the ignorance that still remained
was shown by fuel in his hand;
as he returned, in search of truth,
before his Lord Prajāpati.

[Indra] said:

'This [deep sleep self],
such as it is,

'does not rightly
know itself,
face to face,
as "I am this";

He told his doubt: 'The sleeping self
can't know itself by any thought
that "I am this" or "I am that" …

'nor [does it know]
these things
created in the world.

'Nor does it know any object
other than itself; and, therefore,
it seems quite annihilated …

'It [thus] becomes
a something
that has gone
into complete
annihilation.

'In depth of sleep, there seems to be
no self at all. Does this mean self
is blank or empty nothingness?
How can this be? There's something here
I don't quite rightly understand.'

'I see no satisfaction here.'

8.11.3

'It is just so, Maghavan,'
he said. 'However,
I will explain
it further to you.

Prajāpati said: 'If you wait
another five years here, I shall
explain again; though really there
is nothing further to explain.'

'There's really
nothing else,
other than this.

'Live [here] for
five years more.'

[Indra] then lived there
five years more, which
makes one hundred and
one years altogether.

So Indra lived there five years more;
thus making it a total of
one hundred and one years he lived
a student's life, instructed by
his teacher, Lord Prajāpati.

This is what they say:
One hundred and one
years it was, that Indra
lived with Prajāpati.

When the time came, Prajāpati
enlightened Indra with these words:

To him, [Prajāpati] said:

<u>8.12.1</u>

'In truth, Maghavan,
this body is mortal.
It is held by death.

'This body is mortal;
it belongs to death.
But in it lives
the deathless self,
which has no body.

'[But] it is
the dwelling place
of the bodiless,
undying self.

'Whatever's mixed
with body
is inevitably held
by pleasure
and by pain.

'Wherever life
is mixed with body,
like is followed
by dislike,
pleasure alternates
with pain.

'For existence
mixed with body,
there's no
true deliverance
from pleasure
and from pain.

'Whoever mixes
life with body
seeks escape
in passing pleasures,
can't escape
from feeling pain.

'[But] pain
and pleasure
really do not
touch at all
existence that
is bodiless.

'The real self
transcends the body,
has no need for
passing pleasures,
is untouched
by body's pain.

<u>8.12.2</u>

'Air is unbodied.

'Cloud, lightning,
thunder,
they are unbodied.

'It is similar
to when they rise
from space out there;

'and having reached
the higher light,

'they issue forth
into appearance:
each through its
own form.

'When morning wisps
of mist and cloud
rise up towards
the peace and
clarity of sky,

'they shine revealed
as bodiless,
dissolving radiant
into light.

<u>8.12.3</u>

'So too, this peaceful
[deep sleep self]
rises up
from the body;

'and having reached
the higher light,

'it comes forth
into appearance,
through its own form.

'That is purusha,
the highest [principle
of personality].

'There [in dreams],
it journeys
everywhere about;

'laughing, playing,
taking delight,

'So too, when forms
of seeming mind
approach the peace
of dreamless sleep,

'they are dissolved
in unobscured,
untroubled clarity;

'revealing self
for what it is:

'pure, bodiless
unfading light
of unconditioned
consciousness.

'This is the real self,
remaining always free:

'untroubled by the body
where we falsely think
self has been born,

'with women
or with chariots
or with friends;

'not remembering
this body
added on by birth.

'As a draught animal
is harnessed to a cart,

'so too this life
[here in the
waking world]

'is harnessed
to the body.

'and where self seems
to laugh, eat, play,
to seek out pleasure,
love and happiness.

'But where the self
is thought to be
encumbered by
the body's needs,

'there life seems caught
in bondage:
like a horse
that's tethered
to a cart.

<u>8.12.4-5</u>

'Where sight has
settled down into
the background
continuity
pervading [it],

'that is
the seeing principle
within each personality.

'The sense of sight
is [just an instrument]
for seeing.

'Next, that which knows
"I can smell this",
that is the self.

'The sense of smell is
[just an instrument]
for smelling.

'The eye is just
an instrument
for seeing sights.

'The ear is just
an instrument
for hearing sounds.

'The voice is just
an instrument
for speaking words.

'The mind is just
an instrument
for thinking thoughts

'and dreaming up
a subtle world
from feeling and desire.

'And that which knows
"I can say this",
that is the self.

'The voice is
[just an instrument]
for speaking.

'And that which knows
"I can hear this",
that is the self.

'The sense of hearing is
[only an instrument]
for listening.

'And that which knows
"I can think this",
that is the self.

'The mind is its
divine sight.

'That [self] is truly this.

'Seeing these desires
through the divine
sight of the mind,

'it is at peace
and takes delight
in everything.

<u>8.12.6</u>

'In the world of
expanded
[consciousness],

'these who are gods
pay heed to that
which is this self.

'Therefore all worlds
and all desires
are held by them.

'But, in each one of us,
it is the self that knows

'the sights that seeing sees,
the sounds that hearing hears,
the words that speaking speaks,

'the thoughts that thinking thinks,
and all the subtle worlds
that dreaming dreams
from feeling and desire.

'This knowing self,
this common core
of unconditioned consciousness
within each personality,

'is that immortal absolute
to which the gods pay heed,
by which they gain their power.

'One who finds and
knows the self
attains all worlds
and all desires.'

'This very self,
within us all,
is what we seek
in all of our desires.

Thus said Prajāpati.

[Thus] said Prajāpati.

'Whoever sees and knows this self
gains all the world, and finds
the goal of all desire.'

The self in everyone

What common, universal truth is to be found by a subjective enquiry into one's own self?

The following story from the Chāndogya Upanishad, 5.11-18, describes the concept of 'ātman vaishvānara', which can be translated as 'the universal self' or 'the self in everyone'. As these two translations imply, there are two ways of interpreting this concept.

- The first is objective and cosmological: as the self of a universal being that somehow includes all objects in the entire world.

- The second is subjective and philosophical: as a common, impersonal principle that is each person's real self. This common principle of self is unconditioned consciousness, beneath all seeming differences of body, senses and mind.

As translated and interpreted below, the story moves from various cosmological approaches to a more philosophical understanding of universality: as the subjective ground of underlying consciousness, beneath all the differing appearances of different people's experience.

Translation (from the
Chāndogya Upanishad)

Retelling
(from *FTU*, pages 109-110)

From 5.11.6

They [the learned
householders] said [to
King Ashvapati Kaikeya]:

King Ashvapati Kaikeya
was once approached by a small group
of learned householders, who asked:

'...This same
universal self
which you directly know,
tell us of just that.'

'Sir, we have heard that you have knowledge
of a "universal" self.
Could you explain this self to us?'

From 5.12.1

[The king asked:]

'...What do you heed
as [this] self?'

'Just heaven,
your majesty.'...

King Ashvapati, in reply,
said: 'Tell me, first, just what you think
this "universal" self might be.'

One thought this self was starry heaven,
which rules what happens in the world.

From 5.13.1

... 'Just the sun,
your majesty.'...

Another thought this self was sun,
illuminating world below.

From 5.14.1

... 'Just air,
your majesty.'...

A third believed this self was air,
the subtle breath of qualities.

From 5.15.1

... 'Just space,
your majesty.'...

A fourth believed this self was space,
pervading all that it contains.

From 5.16.1

... 'Just water,
your majesty.'...

A fifth believed this self was water,
flowing into changing forms.

From 5.17.1

... 'Just earth,
your majesty.'...

The sixth believed this self was matter,
constituting everything.

5.18.1

He said to them:

'You, who
are these indeed,

'take in nourishment
[from experience]

King Ashvapati said to them:

'In all these different, partial views
of one same "universal" self,
you draw upon experience
as if you know this self as something
different from each one of you.

'knowing this self
in everyone

'as if [it and you
were] separate.

'But [of] one
who heeds
this self
in everyone,

'as the measure
of all measures,

'and as the
unmixed intensity
of self-discerning
thought;

'[it may be said
that such a] one

'draws nourishment
[from experience]

'in all worlds,
all beings,
all [seeming] selves....'

'But, surely, "universal" self
is just that self which all of us
see in ourselves in different ways.

'Beneath these different points of view,
just what is it that's really here,
shared in common by us all?

'Beneath the many differences
through which our bodies, minds and senses
view the world, upon what common
measure of all measured things
do we rely, in order that
such differences may be compared?

'Our knowledge of the world is built
by joining different measurements.
But on what base? Is there in us
one common base of measurement:
to which each one of us refers
for everything that's measured here
in anyone's experience?

'This common base of measurement
is found by turning thought back in:
to knowing self, from which thought comes.
This is the self in each of us.

'It's the unmixed intensity
of thought that's known as thought alone:
where knowing self is objectless,
pure consciousness that knows all things
as nothing else but self alone.

'For one who knows this, all experience
everywhere is drawn upon:
whatever worlds may seem conceived,
whatever beings may appear,
however seen by seeming selves.'

The rider in a chariot

How can the inner, real self be distinguished from the outward, seeming selves that appear in our conditioned and varying personalities?

In the following translation and retelling from the Kaṭha Upanishad, 3.1,3-4, apparent personality and inner self are distinguished through the metaphor of a chariot.

Like a chariot, the apparent personality moves about and changes in a moving and changing world. The inner self is like the rider in a chariot; it is the living principle for whose sake the personality changes and moves from place to place. But known within, from its own point of view, self stays the same and is in truth unmoved; as scenes of passing world go by, just like the scenes a chariot passes through.

Translation (from the Kaṭha Upanishad)	**Retelling** (from *FTU*, pages 15-18)

3.1

'There are two [spoken of as] drinking the justice of moral action in the world;

'Within each heart, there seem to be two selves, experiencing the truth of moral action in the world.

'[as] penetrated in the cave [of heart], in the ultimate place of the ultimate;

'Of these two selves, one is described as a mere shadow or reflection of the other self: the real self, which shines by its own light, by its own pure intensity.

'[as] shadow-image and blazing intensity.

'The shadow self is seeming ego, acting in a world outside, enjoying good and suffering ill.

'Knowers of reality speak [thus],

'Behind appearances of ego, real self is consciousness: unmixed with personality, unconditioned by the world.

'as also those of the five [household] fires and those of the three Naciketas [fires].

<u>3.3-4</u>

'Know self
as one who rides
within a chariot;

'then body is
only the chariot.

'And also know
intelligence
as chariot-driver,

'with mind
as just the reins.

'The faculties of sense
are horses, it is said;

'and objects are
their paths of travel.

'If changing personality
is thought of as a chariot,
then self is living consciousness
which rides within the chariot.

'Seen from outside, the chariot takes
the knowing self from place to place;
and thus moves on, for sake of self,
expressing purpose and desire.

'But, as it knows itself within,
the self remains unmoved, unchanged;
while world and chariot move and change.

'As known from self, the world goes by
in changing scenes of passing show,
like scenes a chariot passes through.

'Just as a chariot is but part
of changing world in which it moves,
so too each personality
is but an object in the world.

'A moving chariot's wheels turn round,
its body suffers strain and shock.
So too, a person's body suffers
change and harm, and gets worn out.

'Just as a chariot's horses pull
it on to where it goes; so too
a person is pulled on by
sensual faculties and appetites,
towards the objects of desire.

'Just as a chariot's horses are
controlled by reins; so too, are
sensual faculties and appetites
controlled by the intent of will.

'And as the driver of a chariot
pulls upon the reins, to guide
the chariot for the traveller's sake;

'so too, the intellect and heart
think thoughts and feel emotions that
direct the will, all for the sake
of knowing self that lives within.

'The chariot's body, horses, reins
and driver are all changing objects
acting in an outside world,
of which they are but little parts.

'So too, a person's body, senses,
will and intellect and heart
are changing objects, each of which
acts as a partial piece of world.

'The self within is consciousness.
Known truly, as it knows itself,
it does not move; it does not change.
It is no part of changing world.
It only knows; it does not act.

'Its knowledge is no kind of act;
its very being is to shine.
It shines itself, by its own light;
and it is nothing else but light.

'It's this pure light of consciousness
that lights up all appearances,
as body, sense and mind seem to
perceive a world of seeming things.

'Self
and mind
and senses
juxtaposed

'are "the enjoyer",
say the wise....'

'By false identity of self
as changing body, sense and mind,
the consciousness of knowing self
seems mixed with body's sensual acts
and with the acts of thought and feeling
carried out by changing mind.

'And thus, confusing changeless self
with changing personality,
experience seems conditioned by
a physical and mental world
of forms and names and qualities
that bodies sense and minds conceive.

> 'Through such conditioned consciousness
> a person seems to taste the fruit
> of good and bad experiences:
> enjoying what seems to be good
> and suffering that which seems ill....'

The enjoyer and the witness

How is experience known by self?

The following passage occurs in both the Shvetāshvatara Upanishad (4.6-7) and the Muṇḍaka Upanishad (3.1.1-2). It distinguishes two kinds of experience.

- In the first kind of experience, knowledge is mixed with the actions of conditioned personality. And accordingly, the experience is conditioned by changing enjoyments and sufferings that result from the successes and failures of such personal action.

- In the second kind of experience, knowledge is pure illumination: quite unattached to any actions or consequences in the changing world. Accordingly, the experiencer is not an enjoyer or a sufferer, but a purely detached witness: quite unaffected by anything that happens in the conditioned world.

Where self is falsely identified as a personal ego, consisting of body or senses or mind, it seems to know experience in the first way: as a conditioned enjoyer and sufferer. But where the self is understood to know experience in the second way, as a completely detached witness; there the false identification of ego is dissolved, and the true nature of self is realized. Thus known entirely unmixed with any conditioned action or enjoyment, it turns out to be the final goal of love that motivates all actions, and the underlying source of happiness that shines out in all enjoyments.

As shown below, the same passage has been retold rather differently, in the differing contexts of the Shvetāshvatara and Muṇḍaka Upanishads.

Translation (from the Shvetāshvatara Upanishad)

Retelling (from *FTU*, pages 253-254)

<u>4.6</u>

Translation	Retelling
Two birds in close companionship are perched upon a single tree.	These principles, of inner 'soul' and consciousness, are like two birds conceived to live together here, on nature's tree of happenings.
Of these, one eats and relishes the fruit. The other does not eat, but just looks on.	Of these two birds, one eats and tastes the fruit, and thus becomes affected by its qualities. The other does not eat, but just looks on, unmoved by nature's changing acts.

<u>4.7</u>

Translation	Retelling
On the same tree, a person in depression grieves, deluded by non-possession.	On this same tree, a person gets depressed and suffers grief: deluded by a sense of seeming helplessness, and feeling thus quite dispossessed.
When someone [thus deluded] sees the other, as what one [truly] loves, as Lord [of all], as one's [own] majesty,	But when one sees what's truly loved – as that which stands beyond all else, as one's own boundlessness, from where help comes, where everything belongs –
that someone is thus freed from grief.	there one is freed from misery.

Translation (from the Muṇḍaka Upanishad)

Retelling (from *FTU*, pages 196-197)

<u>3.1.1</u>

Translation	Retelling
'Two birds in close companionship are perched upon a single tree.	'What really is a person's self that lives in body, senses, mind?

'Of these, one eats
and relishes the fruit.
The other does not eat,
but just looks on.

'It seems to relish pleasant things;
it seems to suffer misery.

'It seems a separate ego in
an outside world, conditioned by
the fruits of world's activities.

'Such ego, acting in the world,
enjoying pleasure, suffering pain,
is just a little piece of world,
consuming fruits of worldly acts.

'It's just an object in the world.
It cannot really be the self.

'The self is that in us which knows.

'When body seems to know the world,
it is called "self". But when it seems
that body is an instrument
through which perceiving senses know,
then senses seem to be the self.

'Next, when it seems that senses are
but instruments of knowing mind,
then mind appears to be the self.

'And finally, when mind is seen
to be a mere activity
which forms appearances of world,

'the self is known for what it is:
pure consciousness, which does not act
but only lights appearances.

'This light is no activity
which starts or runs its course or ends
or is conditioned by the world.

'As world's appearances are formed
by changing mind, they come and go;
but every one of them is lit
by consciousness, which always must
remain, throughout experience.

'It is the nature of the self,
whose very being is to know.

<u>3.1.2</u>

'On the same tree,   'Appearing caught in changing acts,
a person in depression   a person gets depressed and
grieves, deluded by   suffers misery: misunderstanding
the non-possessing   as poor ego's helplessness
[aspect of the real self,   the non-possessing nature of
                                  the real self, which does not act
'which does not act   and has no powers or faculties.
and has no powers
or faculties].

'When someone [thus   'But where the self is truly seen,
deluded] sees   transcending ego: as the
[beyond ego]   unconditioned centre of all life,
the other, [real self]:   all love, all happiness; there one
                                  is free, from ego's self-inflicted
'as what one [truly] loves,   pettiness and misery.....'
as Lord [of all],
as one's [own] majesty;

'that someone is
thus freed from grief....'

Cleansing the ego

How can the limitations and partialities of the conditioned ego be tran-
scended, in order to attain a complete and impartial knowledge of undistorted
truth?

In the Shvetāshvatara Upanishad, 2.14-15, the ego is compared to a dirty
mirror, which shows up as an obscuring obstacle to the light that it reflects.
But, by understanding ego's falsities and hence clearing them away, the ego
ceases to be an obstacle and becomes instead a means to truth. For it then
dissolves into the very light of self that it reflects, thus revealing the ultimate
truth of all reality.

Translation (from the Shvetāshvatara Upanishad)

Retelling (from *FTU*, pages 243-244)

2.14

Just as a mirror stained by dust shines brilliantly when cleaned;	The surface of a mirror shows obscurity where it is stained by overlying dirt and dust. But where it's cleaned, it disappears: dissolved in its own clarity.
so also the embodied [ego], when it sees the self's true nature, comes to be at one, fulfilled, set free from misery and grief.	So too, each person's ego shows up as an obstacle: where it is overlaid with the impurities of body, sense and mind, which it identifies with self. But when this false identity is understood and cleared away; then no impurities remain and ego disappears, dissolved in unconditioned happiness: where truth of self shines clarified.

2.15

And by the nature of the self, as by a lamp,	A person's body, sense and mind are only instruments through which perceptions of the world appear. They do not know in their own right; for their perceptions shine by light of knowing self that lives within. Light is the nature of the self. Its very being is to shine: as self-illuminating light. It is the light of consciousness, which lights perceived appearances and thus illuminates the world.

one who is joined   By looking back into the self,
with it can see,   one joins one's true identity:
right here, the truth   as consciousness that knows directly,
of all reality: face to face, in its own right.

unborn, unchanging   And here, beneath all compromise
and completely pure,   with mediating instruments,
through all   one knows reality direct:
[subsidiary] truths.   unborn, unchanging, absolute.

[Thus] knowing God,
one finds release:
through all
constraining
bonds and ties.

Detachment and non-duality

What truth of world is realized by discerning the true nature of self?

This question raises an inherent paradox, as described in the following translation and retelling from the Shvetāshvatara Upanishad, 5.7-14.

Truth is sought by making distinctions, in particular by distinguishing truth from falsity. However, the purpose of these distinctions is to find an underlying unity, beneath the contradictions of appearance that result from falsity. So, wherever truth is sought, there is this inherent paradox: of distinction seeking its own end in unity.

By distinguishing the true nature of the self, one is meant to come to the end of *all* distinctions: in the non-dual realization that the entire world is nothing else but the reality of one's own self. That world and self, though seeming two, are only one.

Translation (from the   **Retelling**
Shvetāshvatara Upanishad)   (from *FTU*, pages 259-261)

<u>5.7</u>

The doer of actions   Each doer acts and meets reaction,
which bear fruit   and thus gets to be conditioned
is that [in us] which is   by resulting qualities.
conditioned by qualities.

That [doer] is as well
the implied enjoyer of
its own accomplishments.

That [doer in us]
is what assumes
all forms of world.

It's that to which
the three qualities
are attributed.

It's that [in us]
which follows
the three paths.

It is life's
ruling principle,
journeying throughout
by its own actions.

Each doing personality
experiences conditioning
that follows from its previous acts.

Accordingly, it's the enjoyer
of its past accomplishments,
as it is shaped through various forms
of seeming world that it perceives.

In every one of us, the doer
is the ruling principle
of life that journeys on through time
by its own actions in the world.

5.8

Represented
[in one's person]

by the measure
of a thumb,

it appears
[by its own light]
just like the sun.

The individual self appears,
in every person, like the sun.

It shines by its own light, and thus
illuminates the seeming world.

Seen by virtue
of the mind,

it's that which is
associated with
ego and imagination
that follow in its wake.

As seen by virtue of the mind,
it gets associated with
false ego's pettiness of thought
and will and wishful fantasy.

But seen by virtue
of itself,

As seen by virtue of itself,
it's like a point, dimensionless:
beyond all measure and compare,
with nothing else beyond itself.

as represented
by the measure of
a [dimensionless] point
at the tip of a sharp spike,

it is beyond [all
measure and compare],
with nothing else
beyond itself.

<u>5.9</u>

The living principle
of personality
may be known

as but a part
of the point
of a hair,
divided hundredfold
a hundred times.

And yet, from it
arise relationships
and capabilities
that extend unlimited
to all infinity.

The living principle of
personality may be perceived
as quite infinitesimal:

as always fine enough to be
completely present here within
whatever finite littleness
may be perceived by act of sense
or be conceived by act of mind.

And yet, from it arise
relationships and capabilities
extending to infinity,
beyond all bounds of space and time.

<u>5.10</u>

Essentially,
it is not male
or female,

nor is it
even neuter.

Whatever body
it assumes,

through that
it's noticed,
cherished, cared for
and watched over,
[with concern and love].

No gender qualifies its life.

It is not male. Nor is it female.
Nor has it some neuter gender
in between, describing it
as somehow lacking vital life.

But, through the personalities
superimposed on it by us,

it's what we cherish, what we care
for, what we watch and look for with
concern, in those we come to love.

5.11

Through delusions
of imagination,
touch and sight,

the self [seems] born
and [seems to] grow,
nourished by
the food and water
it receives.

Fooled by its own delusions of
imagination, feeling, sight,
the ego takes itself to be
a personality that has
been born and grows in many ways,
through nourishment that it receives.

But the embodied
[principle]
continues on
in states of change,

But self, in truth, is quite impersonal:
as the unborn, unchanging
principle that's always here,
in everyone's experience,
within each personality.

As body journeys through the world,
self carries on through states of change:

successively
assuming forms
that follow
from past acts.

and thus appears to be a 'soul',
successively assuming forms
of changing personality
that follow on from previous acts.

5.12

Seen through
the attributes
of [various] acts,

Seen through the changing attributes
of mind's and body's various acts,

the embodied [principle]
selects a great variety
of gross and subtle forms,
along with their
respective qualities.

it seems that the embodied self
takes on a great variety
of gross and subtle qualities
to form a personality.

But seen through its
own attributes as self,

as the co-ordinating basis
and the unifying cause
of [all] these
[various forms],

But, seen through its inherent nature,
as the changeless, common centre
where all attributes are joined;

it is beyond all else,   the self is known beyond all else,
with nothing else   with nothing else beyond itself.
beyond itself.

<u>5.13</u>

Unbegun and endless   Here, in the midst of a
in the midst   chaotic-seeming world of birth and death,
of a chaotic world   it's unbegun and infinite:
of mixed-up things,

it's that which takes   as it appears to take on the
on many forms   variety of changing forms
to issue forth   that seemingly condition it,
as everything.   creating the appearances
                                         of everything that seems perceived.

It is the one [reality]   Thus it's the one reality
containing all   containing all the universe.
the universe.

[Thus] knowing God
one finds release:
through all
constraining
bonds and ties.

<u>5.14</u>

It's grasped   It's grasped only by being it:
only by being it,
by coming to   by looking back into one's self,
one's own reality.   from where sight comes, and thus returning
                                         to one's own reality.

It is called 'bodiless',   It is called 'bodiless'; for it
for no body   is not attached or limited
in the world   to any body in the world.
can be described
as its sole resting place.

It is the blessed Lord
who makes things
happen or not happen
in the world.

And it is God
who makes creation
and its parts.

They who know it
have relinquished
petty personality.

It is the source of love, from which
all doing and undoing comes.

It is the principle of light,
from which creation issues forth.

Whoever knows it leaves behind
all petty personality.

Happiness

Value

What is the goal of 'happiness' that people seek?

In the Kaṭha Upanishad, 2.1-2, a distinction is drawn between the short-term attraction ('preyas') of changing enjoyments and the long-term value ('hita') of lasting happiness.

Translation (from the Kaṭha Upanishad)

Retelling (from *FTU*, page 11)

<u>2.1-2</u>

'What is of value
is one thing;
what's just agreeable
is another.

'These different purposes
both bind a person.

'Of the two, it is well
for someone who takes
what is of value.

'But one who chooses
merely what's agreeable
[thus] falls away
from the intended aim.

'What is of value and
what is agreeable
come to a person.

'Someone who
has strength of mind
considers and
distinguishes them.

'So,' said the stranger, 'you've made a distinction. On the one hand, body, senses and mind are attracted by a variety of changing purposes and enjoyments. On the other hand, as these changing attractions keep dying away, they express a continuing principle of value: which is the final, undying basis of all physical, sensual and mental desires....'

'A strong-minded person
chooses what's of value
as against
what's just agreeable.

'Someone weak and foolish
chooses the agreeable,
out of attachment
and complacency....'

Outward desire

According to the Kaṭha Upanishad, 4.2, lasting happiness is to be found by turning back from outward-going desire, towards a spiritual basis of inner stability within each personality. Unlike the changing and dying objects of outward desire, this inner basis of stability is quite untouched by all the change and death that is perceived in the external world.

Translation (from the Kaṭha Upanishad)	**Retelling** (from *FTU*, page 27)

4.2

The infantile go after outward desires; [and thus] they go into the snare of widespread death.	Outward desires lead the mind into the widespread snare of death: which rules this world of seeming things that come to be and pass away.
But the steadfast, realizing deathlessness, do not seek stability here among unstable things.	But those of steadfast courage do not rest content with the pretence of relative stability, sought here among unstable things.
	Instead, they question all pretence until true certainty is found: beyond the reach of change and death, beyond all trace of fear and doubt.

Kinds of happiness

What basis of stability can be found by turning attention back within?

In the following translation and retelling from the Taittirīya Upanishad, 2.8-9, different kinds of conditioned happiness are described as partial and inadequate manifestations of an essential, unconditioned source that lights them from inside. And this essential source of unconditioned happiness may be directly found by drawing back, through seeming personality, to consciousness within.

Translation (from the Taittirīya Upanishad)	**Retelling** (from *FTU*, pages 226-229)

<u>From 2.8</u>

... Let us suppose that
there is a young man:
accomplished, educated,
the most dynamic,
steadfast and strongest
of young men.

Let us suppose that
this whole earth
is full of wealth for him.

[Consider] that
one [unit of]
human happiness.

Imagine someone who is young,
who's open, honest, full of fun,
well-educated, sensitive,
alert, adjusted, healthy, strong,
with all the comforts wealth can bring.
Take this as 'normal' happiness.

A hundred of these
[units of] human
happiness amount to
one [unit of] happiness
for human gandharvas
[celestial spirits],

Much more intense is happiness
of celebration, breaking free
from personal conditioning
that limits ordinary life.

and for one who's learned
the sacred texts
unaffected by desire.

A hundred of these
[units of] human
gandharva happiness

amount to one
[unit of] happiness
for divine gandharvas
[celestial spirits],

and for one who's learned
the sacred texts
unaffected by desire.

A hundred of these
[units of] divine
gandharva happiness
amount to one
[unit of] happiness for
the ancestors in their
long-lasting worlds,

And more than this, there's happiness
of settled, long experience:
which goes on bringing in rewards
for relatively many years.

and for one who's learned
the sacred texts
unaffected by desire.

A hundred of these
[units of] the ancestors'
happiness amount to
one [unit of] happiness
for gods so born by birth,

But this depends on happiness
of cultivated faculties
inherited through family
and breeding in society.

and for one who's learned
the sacred texts
unaffected by desire.

A hundred of these
[units of] the happiness
of gods so born
amount to one
[unit of] happiness
for those who have risen
to be gods by work,

And further, there is happiness
of capabilities achieved
by one's own work and discipline.

and for one who's learned
the sacred texts
unaffected by desire.

A hundred of these
[units of] the happiness
of gods by work
amount to one
[unit of] happiness
for the [higher] gods,

and for one who's learned
the sacred texts
unaffected by desire.

A hundred of these
[units of] the happiness
of [higher] gods
amount to one
[unit of] happiness
for Indra [chief of gods],

and for one who's learned
the sacred texts
unaffected by desire.

A hundred of these
[units of] Indra's
happiness amount to
one [unit of] happiness
for Brihaspati
[the creator],

and for one who's learned
the sacred texts
unaffected by desire.

A hundred of these
[units of] Brihaspati's
happiness amount to
one [unit of] happiness
for Prajāpati
[the Father],

and for one who's learned
the sacred texts
unaffected by desire.

Supporting this is happiness
of mastering one's faculties:
co-ordinating and controlling
them, towards one's chosen goals.

All this is based on happiness
of aspiration to the truth,
beyond all mere appearances
of seeming objects in the world.

And greater still is happiness
of coming to creation's source
from which appearances arise.

A hundred of these
[units of] Prajāpati's
happiness amount

to one [unit of]
the happiness
of brahman
[complete reality],

and of one who's learned
the sacred texts
unaffected by desire.

It's what *this* is,
in a person;

and what *that* is,
in the sun.

It is *one*.

One who knows thus
leaves this [seeming]
world behind,

withdraws into this self
that's made from food,

withdraws into this self
that's formed
of living energy,

withdraws into this self
that just consists of mind,

withdraws into this self
that only is
discerning consciousness,

and withdraws
into this self
that's nothing else
but happiness.

But none of these compares at all
with unconditioned happiness:

where all desires are dissolved,
and simple truth is realized
that consciousness is all there is,
with self and object known as one.

It's consciousness that lights
appearances, here in a person's mind.

And this same consciousness makes known
all objects in the seeming world
perceived by body, sense and mind.

Thus, inward consciousness of mind
and outward consciousness of world,
though seeming two, are only one.

As this is known, appearances
of seeming world are left behind:

withdrawing first through body-self;

then through the self of living energy
beneath the body's acts;

then through the self of mind beneath
the purposes of living acts;

then through discerning consciousness
beneath the judgements of the mind;

and thus at last to unconditioned
happiness of real self,
where changeless consciousness is known
at one with all reality.

On that
there also is this verse:

<u>2.9</u>

'[It's that] from which
all words turn back
together with the mind,
unable to attain [it].

'It is the happiness
of complete reality.

From this all words and thoughts turn back.

For it is not attained until
they fall away; and only
consciousness remains: unlimited
by word or thought, with nothing
to obscure complete reality
where lasting happiness is found.

'One who knows [it]
has no fear of anything.

Whoever knows this simple truth
can have no fear of anything;

'Such a one
does not burn:
"Why have I
not done right?

'"Why have I
done wrong?"

nor burn with the anxiety
of asking: 'Why have I not done
what's right?' or 'Why have I done wrong?'

Both these are only ego's questions.
Neither can pertain to self.

'One who is thus
a knower
[of complete reality]

'delivers up these two
[good and ill]
as [one's own] self.

One who knows truth is liberated
from all seeming good and ill,
superimposed by ego's ignorance
upon one's own true self.

'For truly,
one who thus knows
liberates them both, as
[nothing else but] self.'

Such is the teaching.

One common goal

   Through all our differing desires for various different things, is there some
common principle that we all seek?

In the following passage from the Kena Upanishad, 4.4-6, this common principle is described as 'tad-vanam': which literally means 'that-desired' or, to elaborate a little, 'that which all desire seeks'.

Translation (from the Kena Upanishad)	**Retelling** (from *FTU*, page 140)

4.4

Of that there is this teaching. It is this, which is said to have flashed out and vanished back in lightning.	Objectively, seen from the world created by our faculties of outward sense, truth seems to shine only in blinding flashes of divine illumination that immediately dissolve all sense of the created universe, thus passing on from changing time.
This with regard to the gods.	

4.5

Now with regard to self: it is that to which this mind moves as it were;	Subjectively, seen where the mind turns back to self from which it comes, truth is at once both goal and base.
and by it this [mind's] conception carries on remembering.	It's that to which all mind aspires, and that on which all mind depends: as it appears to carry on through changing time, enabling world to be conceived by seeming mind from fragments of past memory.

4.6

It is just that called 'tad-vanam' ['that-which-is-desired'].	Truth is just that which is desired beneath all seeming goals of mind.

It is to be heeded
as 'tad-vanam'.

It's that which all desire seeks,
and it should thus be understood:
beneath the many different forms
imagined by our partial minds
to represent the truth they seek.

He who thus knows this,
him all beings seek.

Whoever knows this truth of love
is loved, in truth, by everyone.

Love

In the following passage from the Brihadāraṇyaka Upanishad (4.5.6-7), the common goal of all desire is identified as each person's real self.

Translation (from the
Brihadāraṇyaka Upanishad)

Retelling
(from *FTU*, pages 95-96)

<u>4.5.6</u>

'It isn't really for
love of a husband
that a husband
becomes loved.

'What does a wife love in her husband?
Is it just that he's a husband?
If it's that, it isn't love.
All she can love in him is self.

'But it's for love
of the self
that a husband
becomes loved.

'It isn't really for
love of a wife
that a wife
comes to be loved.

'And when a husband loves his wife,
is it love if she's just a wife?
All he can love in her is self.

'But it's for love
of the self
that a wife
comes to be loved.

'It isn't really for
love of sons
that sons
come to be loved.

'So also love of children, friends,
living creatures, places, objects,
love of power, love of knowledge.
All that's loved is only self.

'But it's for love
of the self
that sons
come to be loved.

[And similarly in
subsequent passages,
with 'sons' substituted by:
'wealth', 'cattle',
'the brahmin',
'the nobleman',
'worlds',
'gods', 'the Vedas',
'beings',
'everything'.]

'Essentially,
it is the self
that's to be seen,
that's to be heard,
and thought about
and reflected on.

'Maitreyī,
when self is seen,
is heard,
is thought about,
is reflected on,

'then all this
[entire universe]
is known.

'When this self is seen and known,
then all the world is truly known
and there is nothing else to know.

<u>4.5.7</u>

'Brahminhood
forsakes one who
knows of brahminhood
as other than the self.

'Nobility forsakes one
who knows of nobility
as other than the self.

'Where learning is not realized
as self, such learning cannot last.
Where power is not realized
as self, nor can such power stay.

'The worlds forsake one
who knows of worlds
as other than the self.

'The gods forsake one
who knows of gods
as other than the self.

'The Vedas forsake one
who knows of the Vedas
as other than the self.

'Beings forsake one
who knows of beings
as other than the self.

'Everything forsakes one
who knows of everything
as other than the self.

'This brahminhood,
this nobility, these worlds,
these gods, these Vedas,
these beings,

'all of this,
is what self is....'

'Where worlds or gods or living things
or any other things are not
realized as self; such alien things
must part from self in course of time,
must be obscured and disappear,
must seem unstable, seem unsure,
must seem to change and pass away.

'In truth all learning, power, worlds,
gods, living things and all things else
are nothing other than the self....'

Desire's end

In the following translation and retelling from the Brihadāraṇyaka Upanishad, 4.3.21, each person's real self is described as the desireless and unaffected goal of love: where all desires and dissatisfactions come to end.

Translation (from the
Brihadāraṇyaka Upanishad)

Retelling
(from *FTU*, page 87)

<u>4.3.21</u>

'That is truly
one's own nature:

'this that is
beyond desire,

'When unity has been achieved
with someone who is truly loved,
all care dissolves in love itself,
which shines as peace and happiness.

'free from ill,
untouched by fear.

'Just as a man,
in close embrace
with a beloved wife,

'does not know
any outside thing,
nor anything within;

'so too a person,
in close touch
with his own
knowing self,

'does not know
any outside thing,
nor anything within.

'This is truly
one's own nature:

'where desire
is attained,

'with all desire
returned to self,
desireless,
beyond all grief....'

'Thus, happiness of love attained
shows self and world as really one,
beyond all false duality....'

Freedom

In the following translation and (much adapted) retelling from the Chāndogya Upanishad, 8.1.5 – 8.3.2, happiness is described as a realization of the self's true freedom: from the apparent bondage of egotistical desire.

Translation (from the
Chāndogya Upanishad)

Retelling
(from *FTU*, pages 123-124)

<u>From 8.1.5-6</u>

… It's rather like
those people here
who only follow
where directed.

They live their lives
dependent on
pursuing some objective
that desire happens to
drive them towards,

be it a kingdom
or a plot of land.

Just as here [in this
gross world of body],

the state that has been
won through work
gets played out
and passes on;

so also there [in the
subtle world of mind],
the state that has been
won through virtue
gets played out
and passes on.

Those who go
on from here,
ignorant of self
and of these true desires,

are not free to move
as they desire
in all states.

Ego claiming to be body
lives in bondage to the world.
Ego claiming to be mind
lives in bondage to desire.
All that mind and body do
gets undone in course of time.

But those who go
on from here,
knowing self
and these true desires,

are quite free to move
as they desire
in all states.

8.2.10

Each objective that
one comes to desire,
each desire one desires,

rises up from one's
own conception.

With that
desire attained,
one is exalted
and thus comes
to happiness.

When an object is desired,
ego feels that self is lacking
something to be found outside.
Consciousness thus seems divided;
mind appears, dissatisfied.

When an object of desire
is attained; then, for the moment,
restless ego has subsided,
self seems to have been completed,
consciousness seems unified.

Thus, truth of self, within the heart,
shines out as peace and happiness.

8.3.1-2

Those are
these true desires,
overlaid with falsity.

Though they are true
in themselves,
there is an overlay
of falsity.

For, whatever of one's
[friends or possessions]
departs from here,

one does not get
to see that [friend or
possession] here.

But though achievement of desire
brings a state of happiness,
such happiness can never last;

for ego rises up again,
inherently dissatisfied,
and seeks some further alien thing.

All of ego's life and actions
are dependent on the self;
which, through seeming self-deception,
ego does not understand.

Yet, whatever one
may long for,

of those alive here
or departed,

and whatever else
one wants but doesn't get;

all that one finds
by going here
[into one's own self].

For they are here:
one's true desires,
overlaid by falsity.

Just as those who
do not know the land
may journey back
and forth repeatedly

over a buried
golden treasure,

and yet not discover it;

so also all these creatures
go, day after day,

into the state
of absolute,
uncompromised reality,

and do not find it.

For they are kept
from [seeing] it
by [self-deceiving] falsity.

Self is thus a buried treasure
ego keeps on walking over,
vainly feeling needs and wants
for things that seem outside itself.

Always seeking alien objects,
ego does not understand
that the goal of all desire
is true self, within the heart;
for all reality is here.

The ground of all reality

How does the conditioned world relate to the unconditioned happiness of
real self?

In the following passage from the Taittirīya Upanishad, 3.6, happiness is
described as the complete reality that underlies all experience of the entire

world. For this 'happiness' is the final principle of value which motivates all perceptions, thoughts and feelings; and it thus always underlies whatever is perceived or thought about or felt, through all experience of the apparent world.

Translation (from the Taittirīya Upanishad)	**Retelling** (from *FTU*, page 233)

<u>From 3.6</u>

'Happiness is complete reality.	'Reality is nothing else but unconditioned happiness:
'For it is essentially from happiness, that these beings are born.	'where falsity has been removed from consciousness, which is thus known at one with all reality.
'By happiness, born beings live;	'From unconditioned happiness, rise all of our experiences.
'[and] into happiness those that depart dissolve.'...	'On it, each one of them depends. It's what they want. It's where they go.
	'It is the self that knows in us and all we ever really know.'

Non-duality

In the following translation and retelling from the Brihadāraṇyaka Upanishad, 4.3.32, happiness is described as non-dual consciousness: where all the reality of world is known as self, and there is no division left between what knows and what is known.

Translation (from the Brihadāraṇyaka Upanishad)	**Retelling** (from *FTU*, page 89)

<u>From 4.3.32</u>

'The fluctuating ocean [of the seeming world],	'As all waves are only water, so all seeming things are self, which knows all things as but itself, as undivided happiness.'
'with all its many, changing waves,	

'turns out to be
one single see-er,
without duality.

'This is the state
of the absolute....

'This is one's
highest attainment.

'This is one's
highest fulfilment.

'This is one's
highest state.

'This is one's
highest happiness.

'[All] other things,
that have but come to be,
subsist upon
only a measure
of this happiness....'

The three states

The syllable 'Om' is often used as a mantra or chanted sound in traditional practices of ritual and meditation. But it is also a condensed formula for a reasoned, philosophical enquiry into the three states of waking, dream and deep sleep: as described in the following translation and retelling of the Māṇḍūkya Upanishad.

Translation (from the Māṇḍūkya Upanishad)	**Retelling** (from *FTU*, pages 202-206)

1

The syllable 'Om'
is all this.

Its further explanation is:

What was, what is
and what will be;
all that is described
by just the syllable 'Om'.

And all else,
transcending
threefold time,
that too is just
the syllable 'Om'.

The word that's spoken out as 'Om',
when rightly understood, shows all
experience: all that is, all that
ever was, all that will be.

And thus it shows unchanging truth;
which stays the same, beyond all time,
in everything that seems to be.

2

For everything
is this
complete reality.

This self
is all reality.

Within each person's mind and heart,
while objects seem to come and go,
the self that knows all seeming change
must carry on. It's always here,
in everything we seem to know.

This self is all reality.

This same self
has four quarters.

Reality and self, though one,
seem to appear as different things,
in different states of consciousness.

3

The outward-knowing
waking state,

The outside world seems to appear
in what we call the 'waking state'.

with seven limbs
and nineteen faces,

Here, consciousness seems outward bound:
from self, through little body's gross
perceptions, out into a world

experiencing
gross [objects];

containing all our bodies and
the many other object-things

this is the first aspect,
of universality.

our outward senses seem to know.

4

The dream state,
inward-knowing,

But when attention seems to turn
back in, away from outside things,
to thoughts and feelings in our minds,

with seven limbs
and nineteen faces,

another state appears, called 'dream'.

experiencing
subtlety;

Here, consciousness remains within
our minds; and all that can appear
are subtle forms of changing mind,

this is the second aspect,
of burning energy.

created by imagining.

5

Where one who sleeps
desires no desire at all,
nor sees any dream;
that is deep sleep.

When mind subsides and dreams dissolve,
there comes a state we call 'deep sleep':
where seeming things do not appear.

The deep sleep state,
where unity
has been attained,

Here, consciousness is shown for what
it is, unmixed with seeming things,
beneath all mere appearances
of name and form and quality.

whose content is
pure consciousness
and happiness,

experiencing happiness,
[the inner light]
that's manifested
in the mind;

this is the third aspect,
of consciousness.

In depth of sleep, all bonds are loosed.
All conflicts, all divisions end.

Thus, consciousness is clarified;
and its true nature shines as peace,
as undivided unity,
as unconditioned happiness.

6

This is the Lord of all.

This is the
knower of all.

This is the
inner controller.

This is the source of all,
the origin and
dissolution
of those
that have become.

All things are known by consciousness.

It is the underlying ground:
from which all seeming things arise;
on which they stand, relate together,
are controlled; and finally,
in which all seeming things dissolve.

7

Not knowing inward,
nor knowing outward,
nor knowing both
[inward and outward];

not just containing
consciousness,
not knowing
or unknowing;

Since consciousness continues through
all states that we experience;

it can't in truth be called a state:
in which some seeming thing is known
or is unknown or partly known.

It is the background of all states:
the background of reality,
against which seeming things are known.

And it is also knowing self:
which lights all seeming things, by its
own self-illuminating light.

not seen,

Unseen by mind or any sense,
it lights all mind and every sense,
and all that is experienced.

It is itself pure knowing light.

This is its nature as it is;
to know, it does not need to act.

never the object
of any transaction,

Its knowledge is no kind of act:
that may be started up or stopped,
or be directed or attached
to changing objects in the world.

ungraspable,
unsigned,
unthinkable,
unrepresentable;

It only knows. It does not act.
Its knowledge is quite unattached.

It can't be grasped, nor quite expressed,
described, or pointed out, by
any physical or mental act.

the one
self-evident principle,
where all appearance
comes to rest;

The only way it can be known
is through its own self-evidence:
as the essential basis where
all differences must be resolved.

at peace,
in unaffected happiness
beyond duality;

It is the source of peace and love,
where self and world are known as one.

it is conceived
as the fourth.

It is the self.

It's that which
[each of us]
needs to know.

<u>8</u>

That which is this self
corresponds
to the syllable 'Om',
considered as
a single sound.

Three letters, joined in single sound,
make up the word pronounced as 'Om'.
First comes the letter 'a', then 'u',
then 'm'; together, they form 'Om'.

Considering the elements,

the aspects [of the self]
correspond
to the elements
[of sound],

and the elements
correspond
to the aspects.

[The elements are]
the letter 'a',
the letter 'u',
the letter 'ma'.

9

[The aspect] of
universality and
the waking state

correspond to
the first element,
the letter 'a':

either from 'āpti'
['attaining'], or from
'ādimattva' ['being first'].

One who knows thus
essentially attains
all desires
and becomes the first.

'A' represents the waking world
that body's outward senses see.

This is the world of 'common sense',
from which we start to look for truth
that stays the same through changing views,

through various different sights and sounds
and other such appearances
perceived from different points of view.

10

[The aspect] of
burning fire and
the dream state

correspond to
the second element,
the letter 'u':

'U' represents the subtle forms
we dream within our changing minds,
conceiving thoughts and fantasies
urged on by feeling and desire.

either from 'utkarsha'
['elevation'], or from
'ubhayatva' ['being both'].

One who knows thus
truly elevates
the tradition
of knowledge

and becomes
even-handed.

No one in his family
comes to be ignorant
of reality.

Thus we imagine high ideals,
in search of deeper, subtler truths
beneath the gross appearances
our outward senses seem to see.

11

[The aspect] of
consciousness and
the deep sleep state

correspond to
the third element,
the letter 'ma':

either from 'miti'
['measuring' or
'constructing'],

or from 'apiti'
['merging'].

'M' represents the merging place
where consciousness shines out as peace,
when dreams dissolve in depth of sleep.

From this pure ground of consciousness,
all qualities, all names, all forms
arise, and seem to show a world
outside our senses and our minds.

Whenever anything appears,
it must be known by consciousness.

Nothing ever can appear
without support from consciousness.

Thus, each apparent object and
the whole apparent universe
must rest upon this knowing ground
that's here, in all appearances.

One who knows thus
takes the essential
measure of all this,
and is absorbed
[into complete reality].

And then, as world's appearances
are understood, all forms and names
and qualities return to ground,
absorbed again in consciousness.

12

The fourth [aspect]
corresponds
to no element.

It cannot be an object
of any action;

for in it all appearances
of seeming objects
come to rest.

It is the unconditioned
happiness
of non-duality.

The syllable 'Om' is thus
only the self.

One who knows thus
joins back, through self,
into one's own true self.

The whole word 'Om' continues on
from 'a' to 'u' and then to 'm':

thus representing consciousness
which carries on through changing states
and so contains them all in one.

In this unchanging consciousness
where all appearances dissolve,

no separate ego can remain
and happiness is realized;

for self and world are known as one.

'Om' is thus non-duality:
where *truth but merges self in self
and self shines by itself, alone.*

The divine presence

God and self

From the Vedas to the Upanishads, there is a general movement away from the myths and rituals of religious worship, towards philosophical questioning. In two of the main Upanishads, the concept of 'God' figures prominently; but it does so in the context of a reasoned enquiry into the nature of reality, knowledge and happiness.

Of these two Upanishads, one is called by the name 'isha', which means 'God' or the 'Lord'. In Sanskrit, 'ish-' is a verbal root that means both to 'own' and to 'rule'. So, when God is called 'isha', it implies that all things belong to God and that they are all governed by God.

The Īsha Upanishad adds to this sense of divine belonging and governance, by saying that everything in the world is 'īshā-vāsyam'. Literally, this means that everything is 'for the sake of God to live in'. The implication is clear. God is not some alien owner or ruler who dominates from a distance. Instead, God's presence is immediate, in everything. All things belong to that divine presence, whose home is everywhere. That presence is the single, inner life of the entire universe. Each thing perceived is just an outer habitation of that one inmost life. From that, all governance and guidance comes, in all acts and happenings. All things are for its sake.

Our bodies and our minds are no exception. Each body, each mind, each faculty of body or mind, each physical and mental act belongs to a single, divine presence that is called 'God'. That one presence lives in each personality. It rules each personality from deep within, beneath all outward names and forms and qualities.

That divine presence is obscured by our various personal claims, that our bodies and minds are personal owners and rulers of the life within them. In most of our personalities, there is an egotistical claim: that the personality belongs to its body or its mind. This claim makes it appear that our bodies or our minds are in charge, that they decide their acts and rule their personal experiences. This is a false pretence. It hides the true source from which our decisions and our experiences arise.

Each person's body and mind are driven instruments. They cannot be the real source of anyone's experience. If one looks for such a source, it may be conceived as a 'divine presence', beyond each body and each mind. It is that presence which lives truly, in every one of us. But most of us misunderstand it, by claiming that we personally own the life within us. Its purity of inner guidance gets confused, with the personal and petty will of our externally conditioned egos.

So, in the Īsha Upanishad, a twofold approach is described. On the one hand, the ego's claims are surrendered; so that all changing things may be more truly enjoyed, as expressions of a divine presence. On the other hand, to enable this surrender, a simple question is asked. Whose are these changing things that appear in the physical and mental world? What is the divine presence to which they belong?

And the answer is given that such a presence may be realized as ātman: the real self that shines unmixed in everyone and everything, beneath all names and forms and qualities of personality and world.

Translation (from the Īsha Upanishad)	**Retelling** (from *FTU*, pages 162-166)

<u>1</u>

This [entire universe] is all for God to live in it:	All this entire universe belongs to God: who lives in it, in every smallest bit of it.
whatever changes in this changing world.	Thus giving up all things to God, whatever changes in this changing universe may be enjoyed:
By that renunciation, [all of it] may be enjoyed.	
But do not covet [it].	untainted by possessiveness, uncompromised by wanting it.
For whose is any property?	Whatever there may be to claim, to whom, in truth, does it belong?

<u>4</u>

There is no movement in the one, whose quickness far surpasses thought.	It is unmoving unity; yet mind and sense cannot catch up with it. They always lag behind.

It's that which always
goes before,
beyond the reach
of sense and mind.

Outrunning alien things
which run on by
[pursued or in pursuit],

it stands at rest
[within itself].

On it, all change
and movement
are produced,
from subtle energy.

It is the unchanged base of change,
still centre of all happiness
which every action seeks to reach.
And yet, it always stays ahead.

Just by its nature, as it is,
unmoved itself by any act,
it is the source of energy
from which all seeming actions rise.

<u>5</u>

It moves;
and yet
it does not move.

It does not move; yet it alone
is all that every movement is,
and it is all those many things
that we perceive to move and change.

It's far beyond
the furthest reach
of space and time;
and yet it is
immediate, forever close,
inseparably present here.

To sense and mind, it's far beyond
the furthest distances of space,
much prior to the early past,
more final than the end of time.
Yet nothing else can be so close.

It's here inside,
in everything;

It's here and now: in every sight,
in every sound and smell and taste,
in every touch, in every thought
and feeling, in each mind and heart.

It is the only thing that's known
immediately; because it is
the living centre of each heart:
the knowing self we each call 'I'.

This knowing self is consciousness:
the background of appearances
that are perceived by sense and mind.

It stays through all experience,
as seeming objects come and go.

yet it is outside
all of this.

It is beyond all seeming things,
beyond the changing universe
that mind and senses seem to see.
And yet, it can be found within
each object in this seeming world.

Each seeming object that we know
is known combined with consciousness;
and thus combined with consciousness
is but a part of consciousness.

In truth, each object that we know
is nothing else but consciousness.

Though mind and sense seem to perceive
external objects in the world,
the self, in truth, knows everything
as nothing else but consciousness.

Thus, in each object, what we call
'reality' is consciousness:
which is the nature of the self.

As mind and sense see seeming things,
the self, in truth, knows but itself.

And that is plain reality:
which is beyond all seeming things;
yet always *is*, in every thing.

6

For one who sees
all beings in
pure self alone,

and just this self
in everyone
and everything,

False ego is a seeming self:
a self that seems conditioned as
a little mind or body, which
is part of a much larger world.

Beneath this false identity,
of self with body or with mind,

the real self is utterly
impersonal; it is the base
of consciousness, upon which all
conditions are compared and known.

It is the unconditioned base
of all conditions in the world.

Where outward-seeming consciousness
is turned back in, towards its source,
it is dissolved in truth of self,
which is complete reality.

For everything is known in self,
and self is known in everything.

there's nothing found
not to accept.

There's nothing alien
anywhere, from which
to hide or shrink away.

When this plain truth is realized,
what is there then to be renounced?
How can disharmony arise?

Z

There, in that knowing
where all things,
all beings

are but self alone,

what could
be found inadequate?

Where knowing is identity
of knowing self with what is known,
there known and knower are but one;

with nothing alien in between
that could obscure plain simple truth:
thus making knowledge incomplete,
creating partiality,
distorted views and nagging doubt.

For self, to know is just to be.
Its very being is to shine.

Its nature is to light itself,
without an intervening act
that could divide it from itself
or could obscure its clarity.

Then what dissatisfaction or delusion could apply at all: in seeing that pure unity?	What grief, delusion can exist for one who knows true unity, where everything is one with self?

<u>8</u>

That [self] shines pure, through everything:	True self is pure, unbodied light of unconditioned consciousness, pervading all experience.
unconstrained by muscled body,	It has no organs, nor does it take part in any kind of act. No function can pertain to it.
unaffected by all ill, untouched by any taint of sin.	Untouched by any harm or ill, unstained by misery and wrong, it is the living principle
It's that which sees, direct within:	which lights perception, knows all thought and shines expressed as what we seek through all our feelings and desires.
intelligent, encompassing,	Self-evident, beyond all things that may appear or disappear,
depending only on itself.	it simply *is*, in its own right: completely known, beyond all doubt, as self-illuminating light.
From it, all purposes have been assigned, throughout unending time.	Upon this changeless, certain base, each seeming thing pursues a course of seeming change through passing time that can't be known with certainty.

The rule of light

It is all very well to say that everything is 'ruled by God' or by some ultimate 'self', but what exactly does that mean? What precisely is this 'God' or 'self', and how does it rule?

An answer is very briefly stated in the Īsha Upanishad, stanza 8 (the last stanza translated above). Here, 'God' or 'self' is described as pure light, unaffected by bodily constraints. From that unbodied light, all objectives are determined. God's rule is, quite simply, the rule of unaffected light.

In the Shvetāshvatara Upanishad, this conception is described a little further. Here, there are many references to 'God': not only as 'isha' or the 'Lord'; but, more often, as 'deva'. Both Sanskrit words, 'isha' and 'deva', can he translated as 'God'; but their roots are quite different. Where 'isha' implies 'power' and 'domination', 'deva' implies 'light'.

In fact, the Sanskrit word 'deva' is related to the English 'divine'. They each imply the pure light of heaven, unmixed with the obscurities and the limitations of earthly things. So, while 'deva' can be translated as 'God', it can also be translated as the 'principle of light'.

That principle is also called 'consciousness'. It is the common principle of illumination in all experience. In our personalities, it is seen mixed with our limited faculties of mind and body, where it is found expressed. In the world outside, it is seen mixed with the limited objects and happenings that our faculties perceive. But in itself, it's quite unmixed, beyond all limitations.

Found thus unmixed, beneath its mixed appearances, it is the same everywhere: the one complete reality that all experience shows. It is one single consciousness, expressed in everything, throughout the universe.

This conclusion presents us with an immediate difficulty. If the whole universe expresses consciousness, then it is all alive. How can we make sense of that? We recognize that consciousness can be expressed in the feelings, thoughts and actions of living creatures. But how can we find any such expression in objects that are inanimate, like a rock or a mountain?

The difficulty arises because we think of consciousness as somehow tied to our personal faculties of mind and sense. Certainly, we do not find such faculties in a mountain or a rock, not even in some rudimentary form. But is it true that consciousness is tied to any mental or sensual faculties? Not really. If we take a dispassionate view of our personal faculties, they are only expressions of consciousness. They depend on it. Not it on them. It is their underlying ground, beneath their varying activities.

In fact, consciousness and life can be recognized in anything, depending on how we look at it.

On the one hand we can look at something as an object. It is then a piece of world. It's seen by looking outwards: at some picture of an external world. In such a picture, previous objects of perception are found pieced together; and the new object is interpreted by fitting it in with them. But, by thus fitting things together, like the pieces of a jigsaw puzzle, we don't treat them as alive. Such external fitting builds our pictures of the world, but that alone does not show any consciousness expressed.

On the other hand, as we interpret our pictures, we have another way of looking at them. We can turn back from our objective picture-building, to look at something reflectively. Then it is seen as somehow akin to us. It shows us underlying principles of order, meaning and value. These are principles we share in common with it, at the depth of our experience. As we understand such principles in what is seen, we reflect back, into the ground of consciousness that underlies our pictures and perceptions of the world.

This is how we understand our own actions, thoughts and feelings, when we take them to express the consciousness we find in each of us. It is also how we understand the actions, thoughts and feelings of other living beings, as we communicate with them. For all such communication is based upon a common ground of consciousness.

And we can understand all nature in this way, reflectively: by falling deeper back into our own experience, to common principles that we find expressed within our personalities and in the world outside as well.

For example, suppose a scientist examines a rock, and then reflects upon its construction and its geological location. In this reflection, principles of order get touched upon, as ordered patterns and structures are seen to have some further meaning and function. Thus, principles of meaning and function get touched upon, and even lead to principles of value.

All these principles are naturally expressed in the rock and its geological terrain. And they are understood at the depth of the scientist's mind, by reflecting back there. They underlie the perceiving mind, and the perceived world as well. They are naturally inherent, in both mind and world.

When we thus reflect on nature, we treat it as alive. We then stop fitting bits of it into our imposed pictures. Instead, we listen to what it has to say. By this attitude of listening, we recognize (at least implicitly) that it expresses consciousness.

In the personalities of living creatures, nature's expression is personal, through personal faculties of body and mind. In objects like a rock, where no such faculties are found, nature's expression is impersonal. There nature speaks impersonally, but it speaks all the same. All order, meaning and value are natural expressions of consciousness, whether in personality or outside world. All nature is alive, as it expresses consciousness throughout the world.

In this view of nature, all happenings and faculties are included in it. No happening or faculty remains excluded, to drive nature or to perceive it from outside. In the microcosm of individual experience, nature includes the perceiving body and mind. In the macrocosm of the external world, nature includes all bodies and minds, with all their acts and faculties.

Thus understood, nature includes each act that moves things and each perception that makes things appear. From within itself, nature produces all of its acts and happenings. In this sense, it moves itself and appears by itself, of its own accord.

But as it moves and manifests itself, it inherently expresses consciousness. That is the source of all the order, meaning and value which we see in nature. That alone keeps nature regulated and coherent. Just that makes nature intelligible. That by itself is nature's underlying motivation. As nature acts, of its own accord, it does so for the sake of consciousness. It's thus that consciousness is seen expressed.

Since consciousness is pure light, it doesn't wish nature to do anything; it doesn't tell nature what to do; it doesn't interfere at all in what takes place. As consciousness shines unaffected through experience, it is the knowing ground beneath all acts and happenings. Unmoved itself by any act, it is the final ground of our experience. From it, all actions rise. On it, all actions take place. Back into it, all actions must return and be absorbed. So, naturally, all acts and happenings arise expressing it.

That is nature's basic inspiration. All nature is inspired, from within, by the very presence of consciousness, throughout experience. In a fundamental sense, it's only for the sake of consciousness that anything is done.

In short, consciousness is the unmoved mover, the originating cause of nature's manifestation. That is the position of the Shvetāshvatara Upanishad, chapter 6, as translated and retold below.

Here, 'deva' is translated as 'God' or 'divinity' or the 'divine' or the 'principle of light'. 'Īsha' is translated as the 'Lord' or 'ruler' or 'governor'.

Towards the end, stanza 6.20 is interpreted to show a curious ambivalence about the concept of 'God'. The stanza speaks of an 'end to grief ... for those who don't discern "God"'. It says that this is possible, when people 'roll up space as if it were an empty skin'. This can be interpreted to mean that space and time are not absolute. Their extension through the world is only a relative conception that stretches an observing mind from narrow objects to the entire universe.

When our minds are stretched out in this way, the concept of 'God' arises: as a universal consciousness that encompasses the universe. But when our minds reflect back deeply, beneath their superficial pictures; then all of space and time is seen enfolded there, in the microcosm of one's own individuality. The whole extent of space and time thus gets rolled up, and consciousness is seen unlimited in individual experience. There is no need then to universalize consciousness, through the concept of 'God'.

In the last stanza (6.23), devotion to a teacher is described as a way of love for the divine. Again, this can be interpreted as showing an individual approach, to the same truth that is more universally approached as 'God'.

Translation (from the Shvetāshvatara Upanishad)	**Retelling** (from *FTU*, pages 262-269)

6.1

Some poets,
in delusion, speak
of 'self-becoming nature';
others, thus, of 'time'.

Some speak of self-becoming nature,
or of passing time, as causing
all that happens in the world.

But in the world, it's
by God's boundlessness
that the wheel of
all reality is turned.

But seen more truly, all the
happenings of time and nature act
expressing unconditioned truth
in the conditioned things of world.

6.2

It's that by which
all this [entire universe]
forever is contained.

This truth is all reality,
containing the entire world.

It is that knowing
which originates
all time, holds all
conditioned qualities,

And further, it's pure consciousness:
the changeless source of changing time,
the unconditioned, knowing ground
of all conditioned qualities.

knows
everything.

As moments pass, it carries on:
enabling different qualities
to be compared in course of time,
and lighting all that's ever known.

Ruled by it
all acts unfold.

Inspired by the unseen guidance
of this unconditioned light,
all world's conditioned acts unfold.

It may
be thought about
as earth, water,
fire, air,
and ether.

It gets to be conceived as the
solidity of earth, as water's
changing flow, as fire's radiance,
air's conditioning, and as
the continuity of space
and time, pervading everywhere.

6.3

Doing work and ceasing it time and again,	In everyone's experience, the world is known through various acts of mind and body: rising up from underlying consciousness to take attention out to world, and then returning back again to take in what is thus perceived.
one comes to join through principle the unity of principle:	
through the *one* [principle of consciousness],	Time and again, each person acts; to learn a little of the world.
through the *two* [principles of nature and consciousness],	And every act ends in its source of underlying consciousness, as what was learned becomes absorbed.
through the *three* [principles of quality – inertia, energy and harmony],	Here, where all things are understood, one comes through various partial truths to unity of final truth, beneath all difference and change.
through the *eight* [principles of the five elements, mind, understanding and ego],	
and indeed through time, and through the subtle attributes of self.	

6.4

That which originates conditioned acts	It's from this common, changeless ground that all conditioned acts arise.
and orders all occurrences,	It is from here that different occurrences co-ordinate.
that is their unbecoming – where what activity has done becomes destroyed.	But here itself, there are no acts and no occurrences at all. Here, all that has been done by doing is entirely destroyed.

As actions pass,
that carries on:
essentially apart.

At doing's end, the truth remains:
shown other than the changing world
of seeming acts and happenings.

<u>6.5</u>

It is the first,
the unifying cause
of instrumental causes.

It is the first, the unifying,
unmoved cause, of causes that
are moved to act towards results.

It is beyond triple time
[past, present, future],
seen undivided into parts,

Thus it is seen beyond all time,
found undivided into parts;

shown by all forms,
the happening of
what's become,

the truth that has of old been heeded
as a worshipped God: who's
manifested in all forms, who is
the happening of all that has
become, and who stands here within,
in everyone's own mind and heart.

invoked as God,
standing in one's
own mind and heart,

heeded thus of old.

<u>6.6</u>

[Seen] through the tree
of happenings in time,
it is beyond, it's alien.

Seen through the tree of branching
happenings that form in time, the truth
is known as something else, beyond.

From it,
this universe
is cycled
to and fro.

From it, the whole created world
goes out and then returns, and is
thus cycled and recycled round:
as different appearances
succeed each other in our minds.

The 'Lord' we worship
cleanses sin,
and brings
well-founded order
[that holds things
where they belong].

The 'Lord' who's worshipped with devotion
cleanses sin, removes all ill,
brings order, justice, harmony.

Standing as self,
He's known as that
which does not die,
the home of everything.

Thus known, He's that in which all things
come home. He is that principle
abiding here in everyone:
the self which does not change or die.

6.7

That is the ultimate
great Lord of lords,
the final God of gods,
the ultimate controller
of controllers.

That is the ultimate, great 'Lord
of Lords', the ultimate
divinity of all divinities,
the ultimate controlling principle
of all controlling powers.

That must
be known beyond:
invoked and praised
as God, as Lord
of the becoming world.

It's that which must be known beyond:
as 'Lord' of the becoming world,
the principle that is invoked
and worshipped through the name of 'God'.

6.8

Of it, there's found
no faculty that
causes an effect.

It has itself no faculty
of doing anything; nor has
it anything that it must do.

Nothing equal to it,
nor more than it,
is seen.

Nor is there anything that is
its equal or superior.

Nor is there even anything
that is additional to it.

Its transcending
capability is heard
in many ways.

As the *transcendent* source of all
of nature's energy, it is
revealed in many different ways.

It is
inherent nature:
[immanent in]
knowledge,
strength
and action.

For it is also *immanent*:
as the inherent principle
of nature shared in common by
all faculties that know the world,
all capabilities of strength
and all the world's activities.

6.9

Nothing, in all the world,
is its controller,

nor its ruler,
nor its
exclusive sign.

It's the originating cause,
the overseer of our
overseeing faculties.

Of it, there is
no parent source;
there is no overseer.

It has no ruler or controller
anywhere, in all the world.

Not has it an exclusive sign
whose absence shows it is not there;
for it is present everywhere.

It is the underlying cause,
the common guiding principle,
of all our guiding faculties.

It has no further source of birth,
nor any guiding principle,
found anywhere beyond itself.

6.10

Like a spider,
with threads born from
its primal substance,

the one divinity
surrounds itself
with its own
self-becoming.

It's that [divinity]
which grants us
dissolution in
uncompromised reality.

Just like a spider weaves a web
born forth of its own inner substance,

one sole principle of light
seems to surround itself with an
apparent universe that's made
of its own being, self-become.

To it, each one of us may turn,
from compromise with outward show,
to find all separateness dissolved
in unobscured reality.

6.11

The one divinity,
pervading everything, is
hidden in all beings: as
the inner self in everyone.

It's that which
oversees each act,
that which lives
in everything.

This single principle of light,
pervading all the universe,
is hidden in all beings: as
the inner self in everyone.

It oversees all seeming acts:
as that which lives in everything,
observing all experiences,
itself completely unattached
to any kind of changing act.

It is the witness,
looking on
quite unaffected,
absolute.

Through all perceived appearances
of changing world, it is the witness:
unconditioned, absolute.

6.12

It is the one impelling
will, of the many who
don't act of themselves.

It's that one principle of
activating will, among the many
that aren't active in themselves.

It is that
which makes
the one seed
manifold.

And it's the underlying base
on which one seed of all creation
is made manifold, thus
giving rise to the variety
of things that happen in the world.

The steadfast see it,
standing as self.

To them,
as not to others,
lasting happiness
[is found].

Whoever sees it standing here
through all experiences, as one's
own self, finds lasting happiness:

which can't be found in alien things
that are not realized as self.

6.13

It is the constancy
of constant things,
the consciousness
of conscious things,

It's the unchanging constancy
of constant things, the knowing core
of consciousness in conscious things,

the one
among the many,

the one reality among
the many seeming things of world,

that which
fulfils desires.

the central principle of value
from which all desires arise.

It's the originating cause,
approached through
sānkhya [analysis]
and yoga [discipline].

And it's the underlying cause
of all phenomena: approached
through analytic reasoning,
or through techniques and disciplines
that harness energy and power.

Knowing [that] divinity,
one finds release,
through all
bonds and ties.

<u>6.14</u>

There the sun
does not shine,
nor moon and stars;

The sun does not shine here, nor do
the moon and stars, nor lightning from
the sky, nor any alien fire.

nor do these
lightning flashes shine;
much less this fire.

It alone shining,

It shines alone, by its own light.
Its very being is to shine.

everything
shines after it.

All shines reflecting after it.
Whatever in the world appears
reflects its light of consciousness.

By its light,
everything here
shines back.

Thus all the world is nothing else
but the reflected light of self.

As self illuminates the world,
it just illuminates itself.

<u>6.15</u>

One swan [free spirit]
in the midst of this
becoming world,

It is the one free spirit in
the midst of a conditioned world.

it alone is the fire
permeated deep within
the waters' surging flow.

And it alone is all the fire
of energy that permeates
the changes and the transformations
of the world's conditioning.

Knowing just that,
one goes beyond death.

Just knowing it takes one beyond
all seeming bonds, to deathlessness.

There is no other
way to go.

There is no other way than this.

6.16

It does everything,
knows everything.

It's the originating cause
of everything that's known and done;

It is itself
its own knowing source.

the self-caused, knowing ground of learning
and of all conditioned qualities;

Its are all qualities,
all learning.

It is the time of time
[which shines where
passing time has
passed itself away].

where all-destroying time
originates and is destroyed.

It is the knower
of the primal field,
the guiding principle
that rules all qualities.

It's that which knows the primal field
of everyone's experience.
From that one guiding principle
comes order, meaning, quality.
All things are ruled by it, within.

It is the cause of states,
of bondage and liberation,
in the world
of birth and death.

It is the cause of bondage,
and of liberation from the cyclic
processes of birth and death.

6.17

It is just that
which does not die,
which knows
through everything;

As deathless consciousness, pervading
everywhere, it is the changeless
witness of all happening.

which stands complete,
as Lord and guardian
of this evolving universe.

It stands complete, as Lord and guardian
of this changing universe.

It's always here, as
that which governs all
this moving world.

From it, all order and all
regularity originate.

For this governance,
no other cause
is found.

There is no other cause of
ordered regularity, enabling
us to understand the world.

6.18

It is what comes before,
from which Brahma
[the creator] is set forth.

From it, the Vedas are
brought forth, for him.

In search of liberation,
I take refuge
in just that
which is divine:

the light of self,
within the mind.

In all that is perceived or thought
or felt within our changing minds,
it is that inner principle
of self-illuminating light:

which all creation must assume,
from which all learning is brought forth,
and for whose sake what's done takes place.

6.19

Partless, it is
detached from acts,
at peace.

Blameless, unstained,
it is the final bridge
of deathlessness,
like a fire that
completely burns
its fuel.

It's always peaceful: undivided
into parts, and unaffected
by all action in the world.

It's free of blame, cannot be stained,
the final bridge of deathlessness:
just like a fire burning clean
to leave no smoke or ash behind.

6.20

When humankind
shall roll up space
as if it were a skin,

an end to grief
shall come about,
for those who don't
discern 'God'.

When humankind shall turn all space
back on itself, and shall thus roll
it up, just like an empty skin;

then there shall be an end to grief
for the agnostic about 'God'.

6.21

By power of discipline,
and by divine grace,

Shvetāshvatara spoke
of pure reality,
complete and ultimate.

[He spoke] from surety
of knowledge, to those
advanced along the way,
delighting the assembled
company of seers.

6.22

The highest secret   The highest secret of philosophy,
in Vedānta, as declared   declared and handed down
in a past age,   from times long past, is not passed on
                              except to a disciple who
must not be   thus finds true clarity and peace.
given out to one
who does not
come to peace,
who's not a son
or a disciple.

6.23

To one whose love   Where love for truth transcends all else,
for the divine   so too does love towards a teacher:
transcends all else,
                              who is living truth itself,
as [is that love]   for one to whom the truth is shown.
for the divine,
so too [is love]
towards the teacher.

To such a one,   All meanings that are told and heard
all meanings told   shine forth from unconditioned light
shine forth   that is each person's real self.
from unconditioned self,

shine forth
from unconditioned self.

Teacher and disciple

The relationship of teacher and disciple is central to the Upanishads. In particular, philosophical questions are often discussed by telling a story, in which someone approaches a teacher and receives instruction.

But this teacher-disciple relationship is a delicate matter of emotional sensibility: which could hardly be expected to lend itself to any crude tailoring according to some intellectually prescribed order. On this subject, the Upanishads hold back from their usual style of forthright, definitive assertion. Instead, the teacher-disciple relationship is suggested by example; and its necessity is briefly indicated in a few, rather sparing passages where it is directly described.

Some of these passages are shown translated and retold below.

Seeking truth

Translation (from the
Muṇḍaka Upanishad)

Retelling
(from *FTU*, page 190)

<u>1.2.12</u>

'Examining constructed
worlds built up by action,
one who seeks reality
may well arrive
at disillusionment.

'Whoever seeks this common source
must find a teacher who will show
unchanging truth in seeming change,
the deathless centre of all life
that each of us experiences....'

'For there is nothing
[here, in these worlds]
that isn't fabricated
by some kind of act.

'With sacrificial fuel
in one's hand,

'for the sake of knowing
that [reality
beyond all acts],

'one should approach
only a teacher
who has heard
and is established in
the truth.

<u>1.2.13</u>

'For one who has
attained restraint,
whose mind has turned
towards tranquility,

'the knowing [teacher],
suitably approached,
has taught
that knowledge of reality

'by which one knows
the changeless principle
of truth: impersonal
within all personality....'

Not found by speech

Translation (from the   **Retelling**
Kaṭha Upanishad)   (from *FTU*, page 40)

<u>6.12</u>

It cannot be attained   Mere talking cannot find out truth,
by speech,   nor can ideas conceived by mind,
nor by mind   nor mere sensations of the world
or sight.   impressed on mind by any sense.

If not through one   If not by finding out from one
who says 'It is',   who knows it well, beyond all doubt,
how else can it   and shows exactly what it is,
be understood?   how else can truth be understood?

Learning from a teacher

Translation (from the
Kaṭha Upanishad)

Retelling
(from *FTU*, page 12)

2.7

'It's that which many
do not even
get to hear of;

'You've chosen well to seek this truth.
Not many hear it; and, of those,
not many rightly understand.

'and, of even
those who hear,
which many
do not understand.

'It's only someone
very rare and special
who attains it and
can speak of it effectively.

'For precious few are blessed to find
a teacher who can show this truth.

'It's known
only by someone
very rare and special
who's been taught
of it effectively.

'And even when thus plainly shown,
only a few want truth enough
to overcome the fears that rise
as ego's self-deceptions die.

2.8-9

'It's thought about
in many ways,

'Truth is approached in different ways;
and therefore it cannot be taught
by one who does not know it well,
beyond the ways that lead to it.

'but can't be
truly known

'professed by anyone
who hasn't fully
risen up to it.

'There is no way
of getting there,
unless it's taught
by someone else.[1]

'And when it's taught
as nothing else
but one's own self,

'then there's no
going there at all
[because it's
here and now
what one already is].

'For it is subtler than
all measured subtlety,
beyond all argument.

'This conviction cannot be
attained by argument;

'but, dear friend,
it can be truly known,
taught by someone else.

'This is
what you've attained,
holding so firmly on
to truth.

'For [each of] us,
would that the questioner
were like you, Naciketas....'

'It's subtler than the subtlest thing
that any faculty perceives;
and therefore it cannot be reached
without the help of someone else
who's gone beyond all faculties
of body or of sense or mind.

'It's known beyond all argument
when it is shown by someone else,
as nothing else but self alone:
which different people share alike
beneath all changing faculties
of body and of sense and mind....'

---

[1]The preceding sentence is one way of interpreting the words: 'ananya-prokte gatir atra nāsti'. The following sentence (spread over two stanzas) gives another interpretation of these same original words.

Coming home

Translation (from the Chāndogya Upanishad)

Retelling (from *FTU*, pages 115-116)

6.14.1

'Dear son, it is as though a person from [the land of] the Gandhāras

'was brought blindfolded to some inhospitable place,

'and was abandoned there.

'That person then might wander aimlessly

'towards the east, or towards the south, or towards the north, or towards the west;

'brought thus blindfolded here, left thus blindfolded here.

'How can this truth be understood?'

'Suppose a man, blindfolded, finds himself quite lost in a strange place and wanders, crying out for help.

6.14.2

'And it's as though someone might release his blindfold and say:

'"In that direction are the Gandhāras. That is the direction you must travel."

'Thus instructed and empowered with intelligence,

'Suppose that someone takes away the blindfold from his eyes, and shows him how to seek and find his way.

'Then he can journey on, from place to place, and get back home again.

'he can ask (his way)
from village to village,

'and arrive precisely
at [the land of]
the Gandhāras.

'So also, one
who has a teacher

'knows that he's delayed
only so long
as he is not released
[from ignorance];

'and thence he knows
that he's arrived:
entirely complete....'

'So too, a teacher shows you how
to seek and find your way back home
to your own self: where consciousness
is unconditioned, simple truth
at one with all reality.'

Scheme of transliteration

To make things easier for the general reader, this book uses a simplified system of Sanskrit transliteration. In particular, only two kinds of diacritical marking have been used.

- The first is a bar overhead (as in 'ā'), which indicates a long vowel.
- The second is a dot underneath (as in 'ṭ'). This indicates a kind of hard consonant, called a 'retroflex', as explained further below.

The Sanskrit alphabet is famous for being highly phonetic. In effect, this means that words are written pretty well exactly as they are pronounced. To pronounce Sanskrit correctly, it is largely a matter of knowing the rules, which are very clear and very systematic.

It is not difficult to get the pronunciation approximately correct; and for anyone who is going to use Sanskrit words and names, it is worth trying, because the 'shape' of the sounds is rather important. During the many thousands of years over which the Sanskrit language has evolved, a great deal of attention and care has gone into developing sounds that evoke appropriate qualities of feeling and attitude. It is a pity to throw this away for not paying a few minutes of attention to what the sounds should be.

Here are a few suggestions.

1. **Vowels:** The general rule here is that a bar over a letter indicates a long vowel. Without a bar, vowels are short, except for 'e' and 'o', which are always pronounced long. This 'e' is not pronounced like 'e' in 'bet'. Instead, it is pronounced like '-ay' in 'day'. And 'o' is not pronounced like 'o' in 'hot'. Instead, it is pronounced like 'o' in 'bold'. The list of vowels is as follows:

'a'	as '-er'	in 'father'
'ā'	as 'a'	in 'father'
'i'	as 'i'	in 'fit'
'ī'	as 'ee'	in 'feet'
'u'	as 'u'	in 'put'
'ū'	as 'oo'	in 'mood'
'e'	as '-ay'	in 'day'
'ai'	as 'i'	in 'ride'
'o'	as 'o'	in 'bold'
'au'	as '-ow'	in 'how'

2. **Consonants:** These are generally pronounced as in English, except with the following peculiarities and modifications:

2.1 **Unmarked consonants are always soft:**

'c' is pronounced as 'ch' in 'child' (not as 'c' in 'case').

't' is pronounced something like 'th' in 'thought', but more accurately like 't' in the Italian pronunciation of 'pasta'.

'd' is pronounced rather like 'th' in 'this', but more accurately like 'd' in the Italian 'dolce' or in the Spanish 'Cordoba'.

2.2 **Retroflex consonants are marked with a dot underneath:** This applies to 'ṭ', 'ḍ' and 'ṇ'. These are pronounced with the tip of the tongue doubled back and touching the roof of the palate. There is no exact equivalent in English or other European languages. The best approximation for most English speakers is to pronounce:

'ṭ' . . . . as 'ṭ' . . . . in 'table'

'ḍ' . . . . as 'd' . . . . in 'desk'

'ṇ' . . . . as 'n' . . . . in 'noise'

2.3 **Aspirates:** An aspirate occurs whenever h follows a consonant, except for 'sh' (which is pronounced as the ordinary English 'sh' in 'should'). Aspirated consonants are not familiar to English speakers; but they are not difficult to pronounce. An aspirated consonant consists simply of a consonant followed by the sound 'h': as when a word ending with a consonant is followed immediately by another word starting with 'h'. For example:

'kh' . . . . as '-k h-' . . . . in 'pack horse'

'gh' . . . . as '-g h-' . . . . in 'dog house'

'ch' . . . . as '-ch-h-' . . . . . . in 'beach-head'

'ṭh' . . . . as '-th-' . . . . in 'foothold'

'th' . . . . as '-thh-' . . . . . . in 'withhold'

'bh' . . . . as '-bh-' . . . . in 'abhor'

2.4 **Double consonants:** Again, these are not quite familiar to English speakers, but are not difficult to pronounce. As the name suggests, a double consonant consists simply of a consonant followed by itself: as when a word ending with a consonant is followed immediately by another word starting with the same consonant. For example:

'll' . . . . as '-l l-' . . . . in 'coal lamp'

'nn' . . . . as '-nkn-' . . . . . . in 'unknown'

Thus, the sound of the Sanskrit word 'annam' (meaning 'food') could be described as rather like the English 'un-numb' (if the reader will forgive the somewhat artificial concoction).

2.5 **Compound consonants:** These can occasionally be tricky. In particular, there can be a problem with the 'jny' in 'jnyānam', 'prajnyānam', 'vijnyānam', 'Yājnyavalkya', and so on. The 'j' needs to be pronounced rather delicately and with very little accentuation. It merely adds a sort of emphasis to the following '-ny'. When 'jny' begins a word, it is a reasonable approximation to ignore the 'j' altogether. Thus 'jnyānam' can be quite fairly approximated as 'nyānam'. When 'jny' occurs in the middle of a word, the 'j' is not sounded separately, but only functions as a silent stop which can be approximated by a specially soft and delicate 't'. Hence, 'prajnyānam' might be approximated by 'pratnyānam', and 'Yājnyavalkya' might be approximated by 'Yātnyavalkya', remembering that the 't' must be very soft and only very delicately pronounced, to a large extent as a sort of hesitation before the '-ny'.

List of translated passages

Bibliography

Chinmayananda, Swami: *Discourses on Aitareya Upanishad.* Central Chinmaya Mission, Bombay, 1982.

_________ : *Discourses on Īśāvāsya Upaniṣad.* Central Chinmaya Mission Trust, Bombay, reprinted 1992 (first published 1980).

_________ : *Discourses on Kathopanishad.* Central Chinmaya Mission Trust, Bombay, 1963.

_________ : *Discourses on Kenopanishad.* Central Chinmaya Mission Trust, Bombay, reprinted 1986 (1st edition 1952).

_________ : *Discourses on Mundakopanishad.* Central Chinmaya Mission Trust, Bombay, undated.

_________ : *Discourses on Taittirīya Upaniṣad.* Central Chinmaya Mission Trust, Bombay, 2nd edition 1992.

_________ : *Prasnopanishad.* Central Chinmaya Mission Trust, Bombay, 4th edition 1988 (1st edition 1954).

Cowell, E.B.: *The Kauṣītaki-Brāhmaṇa-Upaniṣad.* Chowkhamba Sanskrit Studies Vol. LXIV, Varanasi, India, reprinted 1968 (originally published 1861).

Easwaran, Eknath: *The Upanishads.* Arkana Paperbacks, London, reprinted 1988 (first published 1987).

Edgerton, Franklin: *The Beginnings of Indian Philosophy.* George Allen and Unwin, London, first edition 1965.

Gambhīrānanda, Swāmī: *Chāndogya Upaniṣad – with the Commentary of Śrī Śaṅkarācārya.* Advaita Ashrama, Calcutta, 1st edition 1983.

_________ : *Eight Upaniṣads – with the Commentary of Śaṅkarācārya.* 2 vols. Advaita Ashrama, Calcutta, vol. 1, 4th impression 1977 (first published 1957), vol. 2, 5th impression 1982 (first published 1958).

Hume, Robert Ernest: *The Thirteen Principal Upanishads.* Oxford University Press, Delhi, reprinted 1984 (first published in England, 1921).

Jagadīśvarānanda, Swāmī and Mādhavānanda, Swāmī: *The Bṛhadāraṇyaka Upaniṣad.* Sri Ramakrishna Math, Madras, 3rd edition 1979 (the 1st edition, in 1945, was by Swāmī Jagadīśvarānanda; the 2nd edition came out in 1951, 'thoroughly revised' by Swāmī Mādhavānanda).

Macdonell, Arthur A.: *A Vedic Reader for Students.* Oxford University Press, Madras, 12th impression 1984 (first published in England, 1917). Used for the original text and for a prose translation of the 'Nāsadīya' hymn of creation, Rig Veda 10.129. However, Macdonell also made another translation, in blank verse. It is the second translation that has been reproduced in this book, from *A Sourcebook in Indian Philosophy,* edited by Radhakrishnan, Sarvepalli and Moore, Charles A., Princeton University Press, Princeton, U.S.A., 1973.

Mādhavānanda, Swāmī: *The Bṛhadāraṇyaka Upaniṣad – with the Commentary of Śaṅkarācārya.* Advaita Ashrama, Calcutta, 7th edition 1988 (first published 1934).

Mascaró, Juan: *The Upanishads.* Penguin Classics, London, 1st edition 1965.

Max Müller, F.: *The Upanishads.* 2 vols. Sacred Books of the East, Motilal Banarsidass, Delhi, reprinted 1988 and 1989 (first published 1884).

Monier-Williams, Sir Monier: *A Sanskrit-English Dictionary.* Motilal Banarsidass, Delhi, reprinted 1981 (first published 1899).

Panikkar, Raimundo: *The Vedic Experience.* Motilal Banarsidass, Delhi, 1st Indian edition, 1983.

Prabhavananda, Swami and Manchester, Frederick: *The Upanishads.* Sri Ramakrishna Math, Madras, reprinted 1979.

Purohit Swāmi, Shree and Yeats, W.B.: *The Ten Principal Upanishads.* Rupa Paperback, Calcutta, reprinted 1992 (first published in London, 1937).

Radhakrishnan, Sarvepalli: *The Principal Upaniṣads.* Oxford University Press, Delhi, reprinted 1989 (first published 1953).

Śarvānanda, Swāmī: *Aitareyopaniṣad.* Sri Ramakrishna Math, Madras, 6th impression 1978.

__________ : *Īśāvāsyopaniṣad.* Sri Ramakrishna Math, Madras, 12th revised edition 1981.

__________ : *Kaṭhopaniṣad.* Sri Ramakrishna Math, Madras, 13th edition 1981.

__________ : *Kenopaniṣad.* Sri Ramakrishna Math, Madras, 11th edition 1981.

__________ : *Māṇḍūkyopaniṣad.* Sri Ramakrishna Math, Madras, 10th impression 1976.

__________ : *Muṇḍakopaniṣad.* Sri Ramakrishna Math, Madras, 10th edition 1982.

__________ : *Praśnopaniṣad.* Sri Ramakrishna Math, Madras, 7th impression 1978.

__________ : *Taittirīyopaniṣad.* Sri Ramakrishna Math, Madras, 4th impression 1982.

Sastry, Alladi Mahadeva: *The Taittiriya Upanishad.* Samata Books, Madras, reprinted 1980 (originally published 1903).

Shearer, Alistair and Russell, Peter: *The Upanishads.* Unwin Paperbacks, London, reprinted 1989 (first published 1978).

Sivananda, Sri Swami: *The Principal Upanishads.* The Divine Life Society, Sivanandanagar, Tehri-Garhwal, India, 1983.

Sreekrishna Sarma, E.R. and Krishna Warrier, A.G.: *Kauṣītaki Brāhmaṇa Upaniṣad.* Adyar Library and Research Centre, Madras, 1st edition 1990.

Swāhānanda, Swāmī: *The Chāndogya Upaniṣad.* Sri Ramakrishna Math, Madras, 5th edition 1980 (first published 1956).

Tyāgīśānanda, Swāmī: *Śvetāśvataropaniṣad.* Sri Ramakrishna Math, Madras, 7th edition 1979.

Zaehner, R.C.: *Hindu Scriptures.* Rupa Paperback, Calcutta, reprinted 1992 (first published 1966).

Index